Thai Home Cooking

Quick, easy, delicious recipes to make at home

The Essential Asian Kitchen

Thai Home Cooking

ROBERT CARMACK SOMPON NABNIAN

PERIPLUS

First published in the United States in 2001 by Periplus Editions (HK) Ltd., with editorial offices at 153 Milk Street, Boston, Massachusetts 02109 and 130 Joo Seng Road #06-01/03 Singapore 368357.

ISBN 0-7946-5005-8

DISTRIBUTED BY

North America, Latin America
(English Language)
Tuttle Publishing
Airport Business Park
364 Innovation Drive
North Clarendon, VT 05759-9436
Tel: (802) 773-8930
Fax: (802) 773-6993
Email: info@tuttlepublishing.com
www.tuttlepublishing.com

Japan
Tuttle Publishing
Yaekari Building, 3rd Floor
5-4-12 Osaki, Shinagawa-ku
Tokyo 141-0032
Tel: (03) 5437-0171
Fax: (03) 5437-0755
Email: tuttle-sales@gol.com

Asia Pacific
Berkeley Books Pte. Ltd.
130 Joo Seng Road
#06-01/03
Singapore 368357
Tel: (65) 6280-3320
Fax: (65) 6280-6290
Email: inquiries@periplus.com.sg
www.periplus.com

Commissioned by Deborah Nixon
Text: Robert Carmack
Recipe Consultants: Sompon and Elizabeth Nabnian
Photographer: Ben Dearnley
Stylist: Vicki Liley
Food Preparation: Kritchai Angkhasirisup and Siriwitayatham Chaidei
Designer: Robyn Latimer
Editor: Carolyn Miller
Production Manager: Sally Stokes
Project Coordinator: Alexandra Nahlous

First Edition
08 07 06 05   10 9 8 7 6 5 4

Set in Spartan Classified on QuarkXpress
Printed in Singapore

A note on the English spelling of Thai words
Because Thai is a tonal language, and words are written in a unique script, there is an inherent difficulty in transliterating them into English. Moreover, the vagaries of accent likewise cause confusion, such as the aspirated "r" in larp, and the silent "h" after "p," which does not equate to the soft "f" sound of "ph." Additionally, Thai consonants are often cross-over sounds, such as between a soft "p" and "b" said simultaneously, as well as "g" and "k." In some cases, transliterations seem to create English or geographic words which bear no actual resemblance to its locale, such as the commonly spelled "penang," "phanaeng," or "panaeng" curry. Hence "penang" does not refer to the Malaysian island. This is not the case, however, with Massaman curry, which is in fact "Moslem" influenced.

Contents

Introduction

The aromas of galangal and lemongrass always remind me of my childhood in northern Thailand. My grandmother would designate one of us eight children to pound the curry paste for the family meal—there was such a lot of cooking to be done! And because my father was a butcher, we were lucky to always have a good spread. I learned to love Thai food from this early age, and the recipes handed down to me from my grandmother and mother later became the foundation of the Chiang Mai Thai Cookery School. I have always enjoyed cooking, and when I was a novice monk—something all Thai boys do for part of their life—I occasionally got the chance to prepare dishes for the religious ceremonies. That was a special joy. When I left the temple I became a trekking guide, cooking three meals a day for tourists in the middle of the jungle. In spite of all the difficulties, this is when I realized how much I wanted to cook for a living. I stopped being a guide, undertook cooking courses throughout Thailand, and eventually opened my own cooking school in Thailand's north.

—Sompon Nabnian

History and geography

Thailand is a large country, stretching over 1,170 miles (1,860 km) north to south, with a population of more than 60 million. While the southern panhandle borders both Burma and Malaysia, and is richly influenced by the Moslem majority who dwell there, the north also receives culinary influences from neighboring Cambodia and Laos, and nearby China and India. Thai cooking is an example of the best of culinary melding.

It is believed that the first Thai people came from the steep mountain valleys of bordering China, settling initially in the broad band between Assam in India and as far east as Vietnam. Although historians have long concurred that this migration happened over the past 2,000 years, recent discoveries of pottery artifacts near Baan Chiang in the northeast date back 7,000 years, while evidence of agricultural cultivation on the Khorat Plateau can be dated as far back as 10,000 years. Revisionist historians claim that the cuisine's historical dependence on fish indicates migration from the Andaman Islands.

Modern-day Thailand began with the influx of Indian traders and Brahman priest–scholars in the second and third centuries of the first millennium. Later, Arab and Indian Moslem merchants entered the Bay of Bengal and carried on trade from India to the Malay peninsula and through the Malacca Straits to the South China Sea and onward to China. While the Dvaravati, or Mon, kingdoms presided over large areas of central Thailand between the sixth and eleventh centuries, the ancient maritime kingdom of Srivijaya in Sumatra colonized Thailand's southern coastal regions. The Khmers, centered in Angkor in present-day Cambodia, left a lasting legacy of Indian-style temples dotting the northeast Isan region. Indeed, the temple ruins of Phimai and Phanom Rung are believed to be the prototypes for the magnificent Angkor Wat in Cambodia.

Culinary history

Thailand's golden age is generally considered to be the 200-year Sukhothai period, from the thirteenth century onward, when the arts and cultures flourished and, most importantly, the Thai script was codified. Some 300 miles (480 km) north of Bangkok, on the outskirts of modern-day Sukhothai, lies a UNESCO-designated historical area of amazing breadth. Inscriptions discovered at the site show that the Thais of the thirteenth century ate a diet very similar to modern northern Thai food today: sticky rice, vegetables, meats, and fish, all seasoned with a nam prik sauce made of salt, pepper, and garlic. What was missing, however, were chilies—a New World plant introduced by Portuguese traders in the sixteenth and seventeenth centuries. Before chilies, Thai dishes were fired with peppercorns.

Thailand is unique in Southeast Asia, as it has never been colonized by a Western power. Unfortunately, this did not prevent European powers from seizing large chunks of the kingdom. To its west, Thailand traditionally held much of modern-day Laos and Cambodia, and as late as 1909, the northern Malaysian states of Kedah, Perlis, Kelantin, and Trengganu remained under Thai sovereignty. All of these were lost to the French and the English, yet Thailand preserved the integrity of its national core, while simultaneously keeping its language and alphabet. It also maintained a uniquely delicious cooking legacy that is nowadays appreciated universally, with some five thousand Thai restaurants overseas. In Sydney, Australia, alone there are more than 250 Thai

eateries, many with punned names like "Thai-Tanic," "Thai-Phoon," and "Thai One On;" while in Switzerland, one of Zurich's finest restaurants is the more conservatively named Sukhothai. Germans are among Thailand's top ten tourist groups, and Germany's Thai restaurant scene has exploded exponentially. Elsewhere in Europe, something like forty new Thai eateries open annually in the United Kingdom and there are more than twenty restaurants in Paris. In the United States, Thai food has doubled in popularity over the past six years. According to the National Restaurant Association in the US, Thai cuisine appeals particularly to the prime demographic group of high-income urban residents with university degrees. And at the Chiang Mai Thai Cookery School, the number of different nationalities attending over the years has already exceeded more than 50—and the last audited count was several years ago!

While the teeming exotic tropical fruits, vegetables, herbs, and spices used in Thai cooking may appear daunting, Thai ingredients are becoming more and

more widely available today. Even herbs such as eryngo (sawtooth coriander) and acacia can be found in the ethnic markets of London, New York, Los Angeles, and Melbourne. But if some ingredients are unavailable, don't let that deter you. This is how fusion food began and how new cookery trends emerge. Green papaya salad, for example, is delicious made with melon, even carrot. Soy sauce can replace fish sauce, especially in vegetarian recipes. If you or your guests have an intolerance to hot food, remove the seeds from chilies or decrease the quantity of green peppercorns. And not surprisingly, fusion food also works in reverse. While Thai street markets abound in wonderful local fruit and vegetables, Western produce such as tomatoes, potatoes, apples, and grapes is growing in popularity there, too. It used to be that only occasionally you'd find an apple variety such as Fuji in the markets of Thailand, but nowadays you are likely to spy a Red Delicious, Gala, and other types as well.

Thailand is the sixth greatest rice-growing nation, yet it is the world's largest rice-exporting country.

While sticky (glutinous) rice is favored in parts of the land, particularly the north and in Isan, long-grain jasmine rice reigns in most of the country's kitchens. While similar to regular long-grain rice, Thai jasmine rice boasts a fragrant, slightly floral taste. Markets there sell many varieties of rice, from the freshest new-season's crop, labeled AAA, to "old" rice, which actually commands a premium price. Like much of Asia—with the notable exception of Japan—Thais appreciate the special qualities and taste of aged rice. Cooks claim it absorbs more water, thus swelling to greater volume, but above all it is easier to cook. New rice, by contrast, tends to turn mushy or sticky during cooking. In a Thai market, look closely at the selection and note the pristine white hues of fresh rice, graduating to the subtle parchment tinge of older, yellowing rice. Broken grains decrease the cost, and rice suited for grinding fetches even lower prices. As befits a country where this grain is the daily bread, the variety is seemingly infinite. Both long-grain and sticky rices are on sale everywhere, as are the "black" (or dark red) grains which are traditionally used in desserts.

Preparing a Thai meal

While a Thai meal can be as simple as steamed rice accompanying one dish—such as a soupy curry or a small grilled fish—the main meal of the day consists of several complementary dishes, again centered around rice. It cannot be stressed enough that every meal's main glory is the rice. The colloquial invitation to dine in Thai, "kin khao" means to "eat rice." A typical dinner should include three to five different dishes, such as soup (tom), salad (yam), curry (gaeng), stir-fry (pat), and a dipping sauce (nam prik) accompanied with raw and blanched vegetables. Try to vary the textures, such as between soupy and dry dishes, and avoid repeating similar flavors. Also serve a variety of meats, such as one chicken dish, one pork, one fish or seafood, and so forth. Moreover, food presentation should reflect a panoply of colors and garnishes, appealing not only to the taste buds but also to the eyes. But, remember that as these dishes are only accompaniments to the rice, not vice versa, the portions may seem small. Noodles are never served with rice, nor do they ever replace rice in a main meal, except when the noodle dish is a full meal in itself such as Khao soi gai (page 86).

When eating a Thai meal, do not try all the different dishes at once. Rather, place a mound of steamed rice in the center of your plate, then take a small spoonful—about two or three bites worth—of any one of the dishes. Eat this in full, then return for a different dish. In Thailand, it is also considered good manners for the serving dishes not to be passed. Rather, the host (or the person closest to a particular dish) offers to spoon a serving directly onto your plate. Note that when dining with Thai friends, they may initially seem hesitant to eat much food. This is a sign of politeness, ensuring that their guests eat their fill before the hosts partake fully.

Unlike other Asian countries, most notably China and Japan, where desserts taste only faintly sweet, Thais use lavish amounts of sugar. Examples range from Sweet sticky rice with mango (page 106), to Steamed banana cake (page 111). Delicately small morsels, often egg-yolk based and poached in sugar syrup, can also be found, particularly in the vicinity of Phetchaburi, one of Thailand's oldest cities. Many of these foods have a distinct Portuguese influence, from the pre-colonial days of Doña Maria del Piña (Marie Guimar), a Portuguese–Japanese woman whose husband, Constantine Phaulkon, was a minister to the imperial court of Ayuthaya. Although she was imprisoned after her husband was executed as a French spy, she was eventually returned to good graces through teaching European sweets to the

royal-court chefs. Such confections are rarely served at the end of a meal, however. Instead, fresh fruit is more likely to be proffered. Visit the market food stalls for mid-morning, afternoon and evening snacks to discover Thailand's truly sweet indulgences.

Harried cooks will value the fact that preparing a Thai meal does not mean precise timing from stove to table. Although soups are always served hot, and stir-fries are generally cooked to order, many other dishes are commonly served warm or at room temperature. And while at restaurants some tart salads may arrive prior to the rice, there are no distinct courses in a Thai meal. Once a curry cooks, for example, it can sit well away from the stove until ready to eat. In fact, the flavors of many of these dishes improve during this slow steeping. During a home meal, particularly, it is considered rude to begin eating before all the food is placed on the table; but this etiquette is less practiced when eating out.

Cutlery

Many tourists find it surprising that Thais eat with forks and spoons, not chopsticks. This is a custom going back to the royal court of Rama IV in the nineteenth century, and while not all pervasive, it is seemingly ubiquitous in the nation's principal cities. Unlike Western table settings, however, knives are not used, as servings are precut into portions small enough for a spoon. Large whole roasts are never presented at the table, and in exceptional cases, such as whole fried or steamed fish, the flesh cuts easily with a spoon. Moreover, Thais eat with their spoon, holding it in the right hand, with the fork in the left doing little more than positioning the food. It is considered bad etiquette to place a fork in the mouth—a bit like licking a knife blade. Conversely, chopsticks are used only when eating noodle dishes, or in some Chinese eateries. Surprisingly, chopsticks actually facilitate holding noodles en route to the mouth. Just imagine the difficulty a child has trying to secure spaghetti onto a fork, and you may appreciate why the Thais adopted this Chinese custom.

Before spoons, forks, and even chopsticks, the traditional way to eat Thai food was with the fingers. This is still practiced today, particularly in areas where sticky rice is the preferred daily staple, such as in Thailand's north around Chiang Mai, as well as in the northeast, Isan. Unlike steamed rice, sticky rice adheres solidly. It is ideal for dipping into soupy broths and curries, or to press onto cooked meats, vegetables, and fresh herbs. Easier said than done, it takes a bit of dexterity and practice to pinch a small walnut-sized piece of rice into a small ball. Only the first two or three fingers, plus thumb, are used. The rice ball is then pressed against a bit of food and the thumb literally pops the morsel into the mouth without touching the lips or tongue.

The Thai diet

Since before the ransacking of Angkor in the Khmer kingdom, the Thais have practiced Theravada Buddhism, obeying its injunctions against killing. Consequently, the traditional diet is largely vegetarian. Surprisingly, this does not apply to fish. It is believed that because fish swim freely into nets, this is not construed as killing. When meats are eaten, chicken is more popular than pork, and red meats the least common. Because of Islam's proscriptions against eating pork, lamb is sometimes found in the kingdom's Moslem south. Conversely, in Chinese communities all around the country, pork is a mainstay. Until recently, beef remained relatively uncommon in a trade dominated largely by Pathan butchers from Pakistan. Even today, its flavor and aroma are considered to be particularly strong. To a Westerner brought up eating beef, this may seem strange until we consider how mutton smells to the uninitiated.

Maintaining a true vegetarian diet in Thailand is easy. Most dishes readily adapt, especially curries and noodle and rice dishes. To name just some of the more popular adaptations, try Penang curry (page 81) with pumpkin or squash, omitting the meat; Green curry (page 70), is delicious with just bamboo shoots and eggplants (aubergines); and Tom yam soup (page 94), made without either seafood or chicken broth, embellished with mushrooms and tofu. Vegetable dishes like Long beans with pork (page 69) taste just as good when the meat is omitted, while Green papaya salad (page 102) is tasty without dried shrimp. (In Thailand's northeast, they serve this salad with salted and fermented baby crabs which are omitted in other parts of the country.) Moreover, soy sauce can substitute for fish sauce as a flavoring, and water or vegetarian broth easily replaces chicken broth. Likewise, omit shrimp paste entirely, or change to soybean paste.

Condiments and beverages

In regard to dips, sauces and other condiments, treat these just as you would, say, mustard, ketchup and relish in the West, or the array of chutneys and condiments accompanying an Indian spread. These side dishes complement many dishes, but not everyone will like chili jam with their fried fish, just as not everyone likes ketchup on their steaks. Equally important accompaniments to meals are trays of raw vegetables and herbs. A de rigueur pairing with dipping sauces, raw vegetable crudités are crunched throughout a meal as much for pleasure as for health. Likewise, the ranges of unusual herbs available in the market make for adventurous eating. Not only are these rich in vitamins and minerals—not to mention fiber—but they are valued for their medicinal qualities. Common ingredients such as ginger, galangal and basil variously settle the stomach and relieve gas; lemongrass has a calming effect; turmeric combats peptic ulcers; and chili, which is rich in vitamin C, ensures regularity.

As for beverages, pure water is the standard accompaniment, although those unaccustomed to chilies should beware: the irritating capsaicin alkaloid in chili is spread through the fruits' natural oils. As oil and water do not mix, downing a glass of cold water to counter its effect merely spreads the burn, rather than dissipate it. A better solution is to eat a spoonful of plain rice, or a banana. Fruit drinks (page 112) accompany food, and fresh lime soda is regularly served in Thai restaurants. Thicker shakes are more commonly consumed between meals. As befits a country whose religion condemns any form of intoxication, alcohol is an expensive beverage in Thailand. Two beers, for example, cost half a day's minimum wage. Since the 1930s, the kingdom's oldest brewery, Singha, has produced a high-quality, slightly bitter brew, both for domestic consumption and for export. It is readily identifiable by the lion on its label. Nowadays, foreign companies entering the market brew locally made facsimiles of their European parents, from boutique Kloster to Carlsberg and Heineken. The local whisky, Mekong, is a fiery brew made from distilled sticky rice. Faintly sweet, it cuts a chili kick, and is consequently a favored drink of late-night truck drivers snacking on spicy and sour sausages, fresh and pickled chilies, and other street-stall fare. Wine is progressively married with Thai cooking, although the ubiquitous presence of chili often fights it. While many contend that a semi-sweet white wine is ideal, such as a Gewürtztraminer or a Riesling, the more adventurous head for red. The only injunction is to avoid the more tannic reds, such as Syrah (Shiraz), and opt for a light Granache or Gamay, or a heartier Pinot Noir or Cabernet Sauvignon. Thailand now boasts extremely limited wine production in its north, but because of cost, wine remains largely a Western phenomenon.

Equipment

The simplicity of a Thai kitchen comes as a surprise, as there is usually little more than one or two gas rings, a wok and saucepan, a few large bowls, and the ubiquitous rice cooker. A wide, tapering knife, or sometimes a cleaver, is essential for chopping, but any Western-style chef's knife will suit.

The truly necessary equipment of a Thai kitchen is the mortar and pestle—these come in two forms, granite and pottery. While the pottery one is particularly adept at bruising ingredients such as long beans and pandan (screwpine) leaf, the granite one is faster at pulverizing fibrous mainstays such as lemongrass and galangal. When choosing a mortar and pestle, the larger the better, as the ingredients are otherwise likely to fly out during pounding. The small wooden mortar and pestles as used for grinding spices in the West are virtually useless for these tasks, and the best alternative is a food processor.

Coconut graters used to be a mainstay in all Thai kitchens, but today grated coconut for milk is just as likely to be bought at the local market, and it is made fresh on the spot. Traditional coconut graters were often shaped like miniature animals, were the size of small stools, and were designed to be straddled so that the user could rub half a coconut shell against the spiked "nose" of the animal.

Steamed rice is commonly cooked today in an electric rice cooker, but sticky (glutinous) rice stipulates tradition: a conical bamboo basket (huat) for the rice, and a deep, narrow rimmed pot (mor neung) on which the basket sits above the boiling water. These bamboo baskets are cheap and available through numerous Asian groceries. An ideal substitute for the water pot is a tall, narrow stockpot. Alternatively, use a steamer basket lined with cheesecloth (muslin) placed in a tightly fitting pot and a covered steamer. Do not spread the rice too thinly, however, as it is prone to become gluggy (water-logged).

Mortar and pestle, stone

Essential for preparing traditional curry pastes, its weight is ideal for pulverizing fibrous herbs and spices. Substitute a food processor.

Mortar and pestle, pottery

The light weight of a pottery mortar and wooden pestle requires almost twice as much labor as a heavy granite model. This design is particularly deep, and the conical design forces all the pressure at the bottom. This is ideal for gently bruising fruits and vegetables, such as long beans, green papaya, garlic, and chilies.

Sticky rice steamer

Unlike normal "steamed" rice, which is in fact boiled, sticky rice is steamed over water, never actually touching liquid. The conical shape of the bamboo basket (huat) is ideal for sitting atop a boiling pot, concentrating all the steam onto the rice. Traditionally, the water pot (mor neung) is a squat, bulbous receptacle with a narrow rim.

Coconut grater

While large, traditionally carved coconut graters are rapidly becoming museum pieces,

Mortar and pestle, stone (Krok hin)

Mortar and pestle, pottery (Krok din)

Sticky rice steamer

Coconut grater (Tee kood maproa)

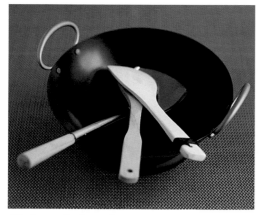

Wok and shovels

Paring knives

tabletop and hand-held models (see also page 56) are plentiful. Merely crack a coconut shell in half, drain the water, and scrape with the grater. As with coconut graters which were carved into the shape of small animals, the Thai word for a handheld grater, refers to rabbit ears.

Wok shovels

Wooden and metal wok shovels are designed with a rounded end, facilitating scraping along the contours of the wok. If unavailable, use any wooden or metal spatula or pancake turner.

Wok

Traditional Thai woks made of brass can be found at some cookery shops. They should be scoured regularly to avoid the accumulation of any metallic toxins. A mixture of salt and vinegar is a good solution for cleaning. Alternatively, use any standard sheet-iron wok from an Asian shop, although it must be seasoned to prevent rust and sticking (see page 32).

Paring knives

Used for carving fruit for decorating and garnishing meals. Available at most cookery shops.

Ingredients

Banana leaves While not essential to Thai cooking—aluminum foil easily substitutes—the presence of banana plants in Thailand makes the leaves a natural choice for wrapping food parcels, before, after, and during cooking.

Bananas Both tiny sugar bananas, about the length of a long finger, and regular-sized bananas are eaten in Thailand. Generally speaking, the smaller the sweeter.

Basil There are three principal basil varieties in Thailand, sweet, holy, and lemon. Western sweet and purple basil may be substituted, but their taste will be markedly different from the Asian varieties.

Sweet Thai basil This common basil has smooth green leaves, and often sports tiny purple flowers. It tastes less of aniseed or licorice than Western sweet basil. This is the most versatile type, used in curries and curry pastes, stir-fries, and also as a garnish.

Holy basil This basil has small, notched leaves with a matte finish, and a very faint aroma of citrus. It often sports a reddish-purple color on the stems and leaves. It is slightly hot to the palate, and is added at the last minute to stir-fries or fish curries, and to spicy curries. It is called "holy" or "sacred" basil because it commonly grows around temples.

Banana leaves (Bai gluay)

Bananas (Gluay)

Sweet Thai basil (Bai horapa)

Holy basil (Bai krapow)

Lemon basil (Bai manglak)

Beans, long (Thua fuk yao)

Chinese celery (Khunchay)

**Chinese chives, flat or garlic
(Bai kuichai)**

Chinese sausages (Gun chiang)

**Cilantro (fresh coriander/
Phak chee)**

Lemon basil This basil has small leaves that are slightly furry and less smooth than sweet Thai basil. It is easy to identify by its distinct lemon essence. Use in seafood, soups, salads, and curries.

Beans, long These are also known as snake beans or yard-long beans. They have a mottled skin and are often black tipped, but this does not indicate deterioration. Fresh beans should be springy. Long beans are commonly bruised prior to eating raw, or briefly blanched.

Chinese celery Straggly and sparse in appearance compared to standard celery, Chinese celery is also a darker green and more pronounced in flavor. Use both the stems and the leaves. Substitute regular celery.

Chinese chives, flat or garlic The flat-leaved chives have a distinct garlic odor. Standard chives, or even scallions (green onions) are similar, but not as pronounced in flavor or aroma.

Chinese sausages These dried, long, thin sausages are sold unrefrigerated in Asian markets by their Chinese name, "lop chong." Made of seasoned pork, they are slightly sweet and are added to stir-fries or steamed. Lay them atop sticky rice if steaming.

Cilantro The fresh leaf, stem, and root of the coriander plant are used. (Also see Glossary page 122).

Coconut milk and cream Coconut cream (hua gati) is made from the first pressing of freshly grated coconut. Subsequent pressings produce various thick and thin milks (hang gati), made by adding water then squeezing to extract the liquid. See also Glossary, page 122.

Coriander seed The dried berries of the coriander plant are used widely in both Western and Eastern cooking, coriander seeds impart a slight lemon flavor to curry paste.

Curry paste A thick paste made by combining the khong sot (wet ingredients), such as fresh leaves and roots, with dried spices. Make your own, or purchase commercially made pastes, preferably refrigerated or frozen, or in plastic tubs or packs. Curry pastes must be cooked before serving.

Eggplant (aubergine) Three types of eggplants are used in Thai cooking, pea, round and long green.
Pea egglants are small and firm. They are bitter, but their flavor actually helps meld the diverse tastes in a sauce. There is no substitute so omit if they are unavailable.
Round eggplants are about the size of golfballs and can be white to pale green, or yellow when old. Although not bitter, they resemble the pea eggplants in their firm texture. Substitute the standard purple eggplant.
Long green eggplants are softer eggplants that grow to 12 inches (30 cm) long. They are commonly stir-fried. Substitute the standard purple or Japanese long eggplants (pictured).

Coconut milk and cream (Gati)

Coriander seed (Met phakchee or Luk phakchee)

Curry paste (Nam prik)

Pea egglants (Makua puang)

Round eggplants (Makua bprawh)

Japanese long and standard purple eggplants (aubergines)

Eryngo leaves (sawtooth coriander/ Pak chee farang)

Fish sauce (Nam pla)

Galangal, fresh (Galanga, ginza, or kha)

Garlic (Grathiam)

Ginger (Khing)

Kaffir lime (Som makrut)

Eryngo leaves (sawtooth coriander) This is similar in taste to cilantro (fresh coriander). The long thin leaves have ridged edges and are commonly used to flavor beef dishes and variety meats (offal). They are also eaten raw as a meal accompaniment or in salads. Substitute cilantro (fresh coriander).

Fish sauce Acrid-smelling fish sauce is a mainstay of Thai cooking, adding both protein and salt to the diet. It is made from a fermented extract of salted small fish. See also Glossary, page 123.

Galangal, fresh This refers to greater galangal, a floral smelling, pink rhizome related to ginger and similar in shape. One of the fundamental Thai flavors, galangal is thinly sliced and added to soups or in curry pastes. When unavailable, use fresh ginger.

Garlic Both white and reddish-hued garlic are suitable in Thai cooking, although the large elephant garlic is probably too mild in flavor. Generally, the smaller the cloves, the stronger the taste.

Ginger A pungent, spicy rhizome, use tender young ginger for garnishes, such as julienne, as older ginger is more fibrous. Young ginger, which is available during the summer season, is identifiable by the faintly yellow, thin skin and does not require peeling. Mature ginger has thicker, darker shiny tan skin and should be peeled.

Kaffir lime The pared peel of the knobly fruit of the kaffir lime tree adds the zest that flavors Thai dishes. Substitute lime or lemon zest.

Kaffir lime leaf Identifiable by their double-helix shapes, fragrant kaffir lime leaves are fundamental in Thai cooking. They are added for flavor, not texture, and if they are to be eaten, they should be sliced paper thin as they are tough. Coarsely torn leaves are commonly added to soups and pounded into curry pastes. They are sometimes available frozen, which is preferable to dried. If unavailable, use tender young fresh orange, lemon, or regular lime leaves.

Krachai (Chinese keys) A long, thin rhizome with a subtle, almost medicinal flavor. Krachai is often mistaken for lesser galangal, which is different in taste and appearance. Also called "lesser ginger." Not commonly available fresh, except in Asia. Bottled or pickled krachai tastes insipid by comparison. Simply omit if unavailable.

Lemongrass Citronella-like lemongrass is a Thai mainstay. The tough green stalks color drinks and flavor tea, while the white portion is of principal culinary worth. Add to soups and curry pastes. To store, stand upright in 1 inch (2.5 cm) of water covered in a plastic bag in the refrigerator for up to 2 weeks.

Mushrooms, straw Identifiable by their closed-umbrella top. Also see Glossary page 123.

Mushrooms, tree ear or cloud (black or white fungus) Most commonly available in dried form. Also see Glossary page 123.

Noodles, cellophane (bean thread vermicelli) Also known as glass noodles. Also see Glossary page 123.

Kaffir lime leaf (Bai makrut)

Krachai (Chinese keys)

Lemongrass (Takrai)

Mushrooms, straw (Hed fang)

Mushrooms, tree ear or cloud (black or white fungus/Hed hunu)

Noodles, cellophane (bean thread/Wun seen)

Noodles, rice (Guay tiaw)

Noodles, wheat (Bah mee)

Oil (Naman)

Pandan (screwpine leaf/Toey)

Papaya, green (Malagaw dip)

Pepper (Prik thai)

Noodles, rice Sold fresh in Asian markets, rice noodles, especially the thinner versions, are more commonly found in dried form in packets on supermarket shelves. Although interchangeable, dried rice noodles should be soaked for 10 minutes in cold water, then drained before using. Use fresh noodles directly from the package.

Noodles, wheat A thin egg and wheat noodle, usually sold fresh, although dried versions are also available. Do not presoak, but boil until tender and drain.

Oil Both palm oil and soybean oil are the principal, and cheapest, cooking oils. Vegetable, sunflower, or corn oil can be used. (The pronounced aroma of Asian peanut oil may be too strong.) Do not use Asian sesame oil unless specified. Olive oil is not used in Thai cooking. Formerly, they used lard.

Pandan (screwpine leaf) Long, narrow leaves that imbue food with a fragrant aroma and taste. Used especially to flavor sweets, the green pandan color is popular throughout Asia, not only in drinks (page 115) but also to tint Western-style sponge cake.

Papaya, green Green, or unripe, papaya is grated and tossed into a salad. When blended with other ingredients, such as a fish sauce dressing, it adds a delicious crunch.

Pepper Finely ground white pepper is often used in Thai dishes, especially in stir-fries. The stronger tasting black pepper, sold whole, is mostly used in curry pastes.

Peppercorn, green Green peppercorns are the immature, undried berries or fruit of the pepper vine. Although available canned and in jars from gourmet shops, try to find fresh berries on the stem. Not only is their taste better, but they are easier to remove from dishes when their hot taste proves too overpowering. When using canned peppercorns, halve the quantity.

Piper leaf Shiny, dark green leaves about the size of ivy. Sometimes known as "pepper leaf." Mild in taste, it is usually eaten raw, but also cooked in curries, or blanched as a vegetable. Also see page 124.

Pumpkin A surprisingly delicious vegetable commonly used in Thai cooking. The deep orange to red flesh of the knobly and mottled fuk tan pumpkin is used in curries, stir-fries, and even as a sweet. Use any sugar pie pumpkin, or alternatively a winter squash such as butternut, acorn, or golden nugget.

Rice Rice is the mainstay of the Thai diet, and no meal is complete without the presence of this grain.
Jasmine: With a fragrant aroma reminiscent of the mali flower, it is the principal grain of Thailand.
Sticky: In some regions sticky or glutinous rice is the mainstay. Slightly smaller in size and more chalky in appearance, it is soaked for hours prior to steaming over water. Sticky rice clings solidly.
Black: Also a sticky variety, black rice is generally relegated to dessert dishes. Usually soaked, then steamed, or sometimes boiled as a pudding, it is eaten as a staple in parts of Indonesia.

Peppercorn, green (Prik-tai awn)

Piper leaf (beetle leaf/Bai chaa phluu)

Pumpkin (Fuk)

Jasmine rice (Khao ham malee)

Sticky rice (Khao ham niew)

Black rice (Khao niew dam)

22

Rice flour (Paeng khaaw jaow)

Shallots (French shallots/Horm lek or horn daeng)

Shrimp, dried (Goong haeng)

Shrimp paste, dried (Kapi)

Soybean paste (bean sauce/ Tao jiaw)

Soy sauce (Saut tua luang)

Rice flour Made from both sticky (glutinous) and long-grain rice, this is a base for Asian cakes and dough. Rice flour is a slightly finer grade than commercial "ground rice," although interchangeable. An even coarser grade of lightly toasted hand-ground rice is also used.

Shallots (French shallots) Resembling clustered tiny onions, shallots are brown, or gold, and, more commonly in Thailand, pink to purple. (There is also an elephantine variety, confusingly called "golden shallot.") The white parts of scallions (green onions) may be substituted.

Shrimp, dried Small dried shrimp come unrefrigerated. They are added as is, or soaked briefly in warm water, drained, then used in many dishes. Either omit, or substitute chopped fresh or canned shrimp.

Shrimp paste, dried A pungent, darkly colored hard paste made from fermented shrimp. Only a small amount is needed to flavor curry pastes and dipping sauces. When unavailable, omit. Also see page 124.

Soybean paste (bean sauce) Fermented and mashed soybeans, flavored with salt, sugar, and wheat. Used in cooking, not as a table condiment. Thai soybean paste is light brown, sold both in jars and in bottles. Chinese varieties are darker, sweeter, and may contain sesame oil.

Soy sauce Used in vegetarian dishes when fish sauce is inappropriate. It imparts a robust flavor to stir-fries. Available in light, dark, and sweet (thick) varieties, or generically as "soy sauce." Also see Glossary, page 124.

Sugar, palm Tan-colored palm sugar comes both gooey soft and in hard mounds. The soft sugar is used principally in savory dishes, and the hard mounds in desserts. The tapioca binding in hard palm sugar also helps to thicken sauces. Often, palm sugar is blended with cane sugar, lowering its cost. When unavailable, use an equivalent amount of firmly packed light brown sugar. Also see Glossary, page 124.

Tamarind puree Although sticky sweet tamarind pods flood the markets of Thailand, the paste and pulp are very sour. The paste, sold in block form, requires dilution in hot water and straining. More convenient is commercially available tamarind pulp, puree or water, sold in jars. Also see Glossary, page 125.

Tapioca starch Made from the cassava root, tapioca starch is used like flour for chewiness and sheen, to thicken sauces, or to coat meat prior to cooking. Substitute arrowroot or cornstarch (cornflour).

Tofu Both firm soybean curd and soft tofu are used in Thai cooking. Use the delicate tofu in soups and broths, and the firm in stir-fries.

Turmeric, fresh Like galangal and ginger, fresh turmeric is a rhizome that grows underground. Its flavor is more pronounced than turmeric powder. In Thailand, it is commonly used to counter the smell in fish dishes. Peeling before using is optional.

Sugar, palm (Nam taan beep)

Tamarind (Ma kham)

Tapioca starch (Paeng man)

Tofu (Tao who)

Turmeric, fresh (Kha min)

CHILI PREPARATION

A note on chilies

Thai food is spicy hot and chilies are freely added to dishes. Consequently, suggested quantities of chilies in some recipes may prove too piquant. But there are easy ways around this, without adversely affecting the balance of hot, sweet, sour, and bitter flavors in Thai cooking. Generally speaking, small chilies are hotter than larger varieties. Substitute larger chilies for smaller ones. Secondly, the seeds and internal "ribs" are the hottest part. Scrape some or all of the seeds away before using. Surprisingly, adding whole chilies to a dish will make it less hot than if the chilies were chopped up. Likewise, coarsely chopped chilies will make dishes less hot than finely chopped chilies. If using whole or large pieces of chilies, simply avoid eating them.

When working with chilies avoid touching your skin, eyes and nose, as fresh chilies contain volatile oils that can burn skin and tender membranes. Apply a barrier cream to hands prior to handling, or wear gloves. The soaking water from both dried and fresh chilies can also burn and cause a rash. Always wash your hands well in cool, soapy water after use, and thoroughly scrub the chopping board and knife. When the taste of chili overwhelms, immediately eat a spoonful of plain rice or a piece of banana, or drink milk. Do not down a glass of water, as it tends to spread the heat throughout the mouth.

Chilies (Prik)

Small chilies: The thin red or green chili averages less than 1 inch (2.5 cm) in length. It is descriptively known as "prik khii noo," Thai for "rat turd." It is the hottest of all, so use accordingly. Pequin or Brazilian Malagueta chilies may be substituted. **Medium chilies:** Only slightly less piquant is the medium-sized chili, "prik chee faa," which is about 1–1$\frac{1}{2}$ inches (2.5–4 cm) in length. A serrano, fips or Dutch chili may be substituted. **Long chilies:** The finger-thick, long chili, "prik num," is the mildest of the common varieties. Another mild, long chili, such as Anaheim, may be substituted. All these chilies are available both fresh and dried.

Chili powder (prik pong)

Made from the long chili, Thai chili powder is not as piquant as cayenne pepper, nor is it equivalent to Mexican chili powder, which is a combination of spices. When unavailable, use red pepper flakes ground to a powder in a mortar or a food processor.

Small chilies

Medium chilies

Long chilies

Chili powder

Step-by-Step
preparing dried
chilies

1. Pull or cut the stem off the long chilies.

2. Roll the chili pod gently in the palm of your hand.

3. Turn the chili upside down and shake out the loosened seeds.

4. Soak pods in warm water for 10 minutes, then drain. Caution: Do not let the soaking liquid touch your hands as it could burn your skin.

Roasting dried chilies

Slightly cooking dried chilies improves their flavor. Put the pods in a dry wok or a large, heavy frying pan over medium-high heat and toast, stirring constantly, until the chilies are fragrant and begin to brown, but without burning. (Note: Ensure the room is well ventilated.)

1   **2**   **3**   **4**

Step-by-Step
roasting
and peeling
fresh chilies

In some recipes, such as Northern-style chili dipping Sauce (page 117), chilies are roasted and peeled to remove the slightly bitter skin and to improve the taste of the flesh.

1. Skewer the chilies on bamboo sticks or metal fondue forks and pass over a gas flame until blackened on all sides.

2. Alternately, arrange the chilies in a single layer on a baking sheet and place under a preheated broiler (grill), as close to the heat source as possible, until blackened on all sides, turning as required.

3. Remove from heat and cover with a damp towel. Let stand until chilies are cool to the touch.

4. Peel the skin and pull off the stems, but do not remove the seeds.

1  **2**  **3** 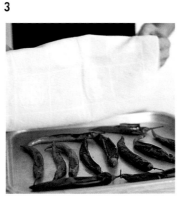 **4**

DECORATION AND PRESENTATION

It would be unfathomable for a Thai cook to entertain without considering presentation, from tableware and flower arrangements to the highly cultivated art of fruit and vegetable carving. Thai cooks are renowned for their delicate skills. While the international hotels are typically where one expects beautifully carved foods, they are far from unknown at home. Indeed, in Thailand, the craft is taught at an early age.

Generally, the most important utensil is a very sharp paring knife, or a slightly smaller crescent-bladed fruit-carving knife. (To maintain their sharp edges, these knives are reserved only for carving and garnishing.) Both are commonly available at cookery shops. Scalpels from any pharmacy also come in handy for more precise work. Knives with V- and U-shaped blades are instrumental in chiseling out engraved decorations. The essential technique in Thai fruit and vegetable carving is to hold the knife upside down, with the knife blade between your thumb and first two fingers, the handle upward, almost resting on the top of your hand. This may initially seem awkward. Carve away from you, not towards the body.

Traditional Thai garnish can be as elaborate as an ornately carved pumpkin or watermelon, or as intricate as a fishing net sliced from daikon or a dahlia carrot. More commonly, fruits and vegetables take on the simple forms of a chili flower or tomato rose. And for an even more natural presentation, do as the Thai home cooks regularly practice: adorn dishes with simple herbs such as finely shredded kaffir lime or basil leaves, rounds of chili, a julienne of young fresh ginger, sprigs of mint, or a drizzle of coconut cream.

Crudités

A selection of raw vegetables and herbs is a standard inclusion at the Thai table. Usually this accompanies a dipping sauce, though these crudités are not plunged into the dip; instead, a small spoonful of the sauce is combined with rice, and the crudités are eaten as an accompaniment. A wide range of vegetables are offered, from baby corn to slices of eggplant and cucumber, lightly bruised long beans cut into 2-inch (5-cm) lengths or tied into small knots, winged beans, okra, and strips of cabbage. Other accompaniments include fried pork rinds, particularly in the north, small fried fish, and hard-boiled eggs, both plain and salted. Fresh herbs are eaten with various other dishes. A selection can include sweet Thai basil, mint, and lead tree (kra thin). Lettuce and other greens, such as water spinach (morning glory), are also served.

Step-by-Step rolling a tomato rose

1. Take a firm, medium to large red tomato. Beginning at its base, pare the skin thinly around the tomato in a continuous spiral about ³/₄-inch (2-cm) wide.

1

2. Do not let the skin break. Lay the skin on a working surface, skin-side up, then pinch and roll the tomato skin into a tight spiral nest.

2

3. Stand it upright, and gently prod outside layers to open like a rose. The center should remain tight like a bud. If desired, decorate with a couple of basil leaves to the side. Store under a damp paper towel in the refrigerator no longer than 2–3 days, until the edges wrinkle.

3

Step-by-Step cutting fine shreds

Also known as chiffonade, paper-thin shreds of herbs are achieved by rolling several leaves together into a tight cylinder, then slicing crosswise. When cutting kaffir lime leaves, first remove the tough center stem. Tender leaves such as basil and mint merely need to be pinched from their stems.

Cutting a chiffonade

1

2

Step-by-Step carving
a **chili flower**
Medium chili

Medium length chilies are ideal for the simplest of chili flowers. Make sure that they are very crisp and fresh, either green or red.

1. Hold the chili flat on a board and use a thin sharp knife to cut lengthwise along the chili from stem to tip. Make about 5 parallel cuts just through the skin to the seeds, but not across them to the other side.

2. Plunge into ice water and the chili "petals" will curl back, while the seed cluster becomes the stamen. If parts of the flower remain closed, prod them gently with the knife and return the flower to the water. These will keep for up to 36 hours if refrigerated in cold water.

Long chili

Long chilies do not blossom as exquisitely as the shorter varieties. To make this garnish, which resembles the beautiful kiriboon flower of Southeast Asia, use a scalpel or preferably a thin V-shaped garnishing knife (available at cookware shops and from some cake-decorating suppliers).

1. Make small V-shaped incisions along the length of the chili, in parallel rows. They should be about $\frac{1}{8}$ inch (3 mm) wide and no more than $\frac{1}{4}$ inch (6 mm) long.

Plunge into ice water, as for medium chili, until the incisions curl back like a flower. Note: For a more spectacular presentation, stick a thin carrot sliver into each of the chiseled holes.

1

Step-by-Step carving a round **eggplant** flower

1

Round Thai eggplants, about the size of golfballs, form graphic petals when cut into geometric shapes. The techniques here show a Western cutting style. For traditional Thai carving techniques, see page 28.

1. Use a sharp paring knife, cut the eggplant lengthwise—from top to stem—into 4 even sections.

2. Score through the skin of each section, making parallel cuts, about ¼ inch (6 mm) from the first cuts.

3. Gently prod the tip to loosen the skin from the interior of the eggplant. The skin should readily open up from the eggplant, exposing a bulbous center.

4. Plunge into cold water with a small amount of lemon juice or vinegar added to prevent discoloration. Use the same day. For variation, cut small notches along the side of the scored skin.

2

3

4

1

2

4

Step-by-Step seasoning a **new wok**

Rolled-steel woks need to be seasoned before using, or food will stick and they will rust.

1. Wipe the wok lightly with oil and place it over high heat until smoking. Immediately plunge it into hot water, then return to heat to dry. Wipe again with oil and repeat these steps 3 times. At no time should you use soap.

2. To keep the wok clean, rinse with hot water immediately after use and scour with a plastic or nonmetallic brush. Never use soap, or you will need to season the wok all over again. Do not wipe dry, but place over a low heat to dry. Wipe lightly with oil and store.

3. When cooking with a wok, always preheat it before adding any ingredients, including oil. After adding oil, rotate the wok to spread the oil evenly up the sides, then heat before adding anything else.

4. Because of the wok's conical shape, a gas flame is preferable to electric as it disperses the heat upward along the sides of the wok. Gas also allows instant regulation of the heat. If you do not have a wok, use a large frying pan, a cast-iron skillet, or a russe.

Step-by-Step toasting nuts **and seeds**

1

1. Place nuts or seeds, such as peanuts, cashews and sesame seeds in a dry wok or frying pan over medium heat, and toast, stirring constantly, until lightly golden and fragrant.

2. Alternatively, preheat the oven to 400°F (200°C). Spread the nuts or seeds on a rimmed baking pan and toast for 8–12 minutes, shaking the pan once to ensure even browning. Like spices, nuts and seeds should not be overcooked, lest they become bitter.

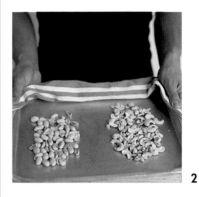

2

Step-by-Step toasting **spices**

1

1. For fresher flavor, use whole spices then toast and grind them yourself. Because spices all toast at different times, toast them separately in a dry wok or frying pan over medium-high heat, stirring constantly, until fragrant. This will take anywhere from a few seconds to no more than 90 seconds. The general rule is to use your nose: once fragrant, remove the spice from the heat immediately, lest it become acrid.

2. Transfer them into a mortar, let cool and then grind.

2

Peeling **rhizomes**

1

Fresh galangal, ginger, and turmeric should be peeled before using. Removing the peel concentrates the flavors of the inner root and eliminates tasteless fiber. However, this step is considered optional by many, and for that reason, the recipes in this book leave the choice of peeling optional. To peel, pare thinly with a small paring knife. While galangal and ginger can be safely held in an exposed hand, wear gloves when cutting turmeric as it stains skin.

1

Step-by-Step deveining and butterflying **shrimp**

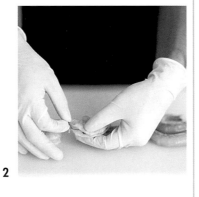

2

Deveining simply means to remove the gritty intestinal tract that runs along the back of shrimp (prawns). Butterflying shrimp is optional (although it does speed the cooking process), and it only works well with raw shrimp (green king prawns).

1. Remove the shell, then use a small paring knife to lightly score along the back of the shrimp, exposing the dark vein.

2. Gently pull vein to remove.

3. Cut the shrimp deeper along the back, but not completely through, as this allows the meat to open up like a butterfly during cooking, hence its name. For aesthetic reasons, Thai cooks do not remove the shrimp tail.

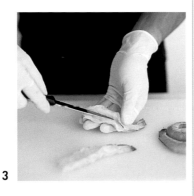

3

Step-by-Step cooking "beautiful rice"

The Thai for steamed rice, "khao suey," means "beautiful rice." Though commonly referred to as "steamed rice," standard Thai rice is actually boiled.

1. Rinse long-grain rice—preferably jasmine—until the water runs clear, but do not overwork the rice or the grains may break. Drain the rice and put it in a deep, heavy saucepan with a tight-fitting lid.

2. Fill the pan with water to cover the rice by $3/4$ inch (2 cm). Traditionally, cooks measured by placing their index finger on the rice, adding just enough water to touch their first joint. Do not measure from the pan's bottom, but from the top of the rice.

3. Over high heat, bring the water to a boil and cook until craters form on the rice's surface and the water has disappeared. Immediately cover tightly and reduce heat to a bare simmer. Cook for about 20 minutes, or until tender. Do not lift the lid during cooking.

4. Use a wooden rice paddle or wooden spoon to fluff the rice up and loosen the grains. If cooking in a nonstick pan, using a bamboo or wooden implement avoids scratching the surface.

Note
Sticky rice is as important in a Thai menu as "beautiful rice." See page 106 for step-by-step techniques of cooking sticky rice.

Hint
When cooked, rice swells to two and a half times in volume. Estimate about 1–1^1/2 cups cooked rice per person.

1

2

3

4

Ingredients

1 whole duck (about 4 lb/2 kg)

¼ cup (2 fl oz/60 ml) sweet (thick) soy sauce

½ cup (2 ½ oz/75 g) coarsely sliced fresh ginger

¼ cup (2 fl oz/60 ml) soybean paste (bean sauce)

¼ cup (2 fl oz/60 ml) oyster sauce

6 cloves garlic, crushed

8 cilantro (fresh coriander) roots, or 2 tablespoons coarsely chopped stems

Thai roast duck
Ped yang

Lightly prick duck skin all over with a fork. Using hands or a pastry brush, coat duck with sweet soy sauce. Let stand to marinate at room temperature for 1 hour, or overnight, covered, in the refrigerator. Preheat oven to 400°F (200°C).

In a small bowl, combine all remaining ingredients, and stir well. Spoon into duck's cavity. Skewer with a toothpick to close cavity. Place duck, breast side up, on a rack in a roasting pan on the lowest shelf of the oven, and roast for 10 minutes. Reduce heat to 350°F (180°C) and roast, turning once, for about 1 hour, or until a leg moves easily in its socket. If duck is over-browning, loosely cover with aluminum foil. Remove from oven and let rest for at least 15 minutes before carving.

When ready to serve, remove and discard stuffing and chop duck into small pieces. This is done easily using a cleaver, cutting through bones, as opposed to carving meat away from the carcass.

Serves 4

Note: In Thailand, duck is eaten well done, though not falling from the bones. When using this meat in another recipe, the duck should be slightly firm, as it will continue cooking in sauce.

Variation

Thai roasted duck breasts
Prick the skin of 4–6 duck breast halves lightly with a fork. Coat breasts with stuffing (above). Let stand at room temeprature for at least 1 hour. Preheat oven to 400°F (200°C). Scrape off stuffing from duck and coat each breast with a spoonful of sweet soy sauce. Place in oven, reduce heat to 350°F (180°C), and roast for 40–50 minutes. Remove from heat, let cool.

Whole fried fish with **chili and basil**

Plaa nin laad prik bai horapa

With a very sharp knife, score each side of fish with three deep slashes to the bone.

In a large wok or deep-fryer, heat 4 inches (10 cm) oil to 350°F (180°C). Add fish and cook until crispy and brown on both sides and opaque throughout, 7–10 minutes, depending on thickness. Using a skimmer, transfer fish to paper towels to drain.

Meanwhile, in a wok or medium, heavy frying pan over medium-high heat, heat 2 tablespoons oil and fry garlic, onion, and all chilies until garlic just begins to brown. Add fish sauce, soy sauce, and chicken broth or water, stir to combine, then cook for 1 minute. Add basil leaves, stir well, and pour over fish. Transfer to a large serving platter, sprinkle over with fresh cilantro, and serve.

Serves 4

Note: In Thailand, fish is served whole, with the head intact. If desired, use a cleaver or chef's knife to cut the head of the fish. Discard or retain the head for broth. For a less spicy dish, remove seeds from the chilies.

Hint: This dish can also be garnished with fried basil leaves. In a large frying pan, heat 1 cup (8 fl oz/250 ml) oil. Working in batches, fry about 20 fresh basil leaves. Using a slotted spoon, remove from oil and drain on paper towels.

Ingredients

1–2 whole fish, about 9½ inches (24 cm) long, such as snapper, bream, flounder, or trout, scaled and gutted

vegetable oil for deep-frying, plus 2 tablespoons

6 cloves garlic, coarsely chopped

1 onion, finely chopped

5 fresh medium red chilies, thinly sliced

1 fresh long red chili, cut into large pieces

1 fresh long green chili, cut into large pieces

1 tablespoon fish sauce

1 tablespoon soy sauce

½ cup (2 fl oz/60 ml) chicken broth or water

¾ cup (¾ oz/20 g) loosely packed sweet Thai basil leaves, coarsely chopped

½ cup (¾ oz/20 g) chopped cilantro (fresh coriander) leaves

Ingredients

1½ lb (750 g) cooked or raw crab in the shell

1 cup (8 fl oz/250 ml) milk

1 egg, beaten

2 tablespoons soy sauce

½ teaspoon granulated (white) sugar

½ cup (4 fl oz/125 ml) strained chili oil (see page 118) or ¼ cup chili oil with ¼ cup vegetable oil

1 teaspoon curry powder

¼ cup (2 fl oz/60 ml) vegetable oil

1 fresh long red chili, cut into strips

4 scallions (green onions), coarsely chopped

¼ cup (1 oz/30 g) coarsely chopped Chinese or regular celery

Crab with yellow curry powder
Poo phad pong garee

Clean crab by pulling off the apron flap on the bottom of the shell. Pry off top shell, remove gills, intestines, and mouth parts. Cut small crabs in half, or large crabs into eight pieces. Twist off claws. Refrigerate until ready to use.

In a medium bowl, combine milk, egg, soy sauce, sugar, chili oil, and curry powder; whisk to blend well.

Heat vegetable oil in a wok or large, heavy frying pan over high heat. Add milk mixture and bring to a boil, stirring constantly. Add crab and cook for 2 minutes, then turn off heat and add chili, scallions, and celery. Spoon into a deep serving dish and serve.

Serves 4–6

Note: Make sure you use evaporated milk in this recipe and not sweetened condensed milk. For a less piquant dish, substitute half the chili oil with vegetable oil and use a mild curry powder.

Chicken with lemongrass

Gai yang

To make marinade: In a mortar, combine garlic and lemongrass and pound to a coarse paste with a pestle. Or, thinly slice, then chop together to a coarse paste with a cleaver or chef's knife. Stir in all remaining marinade ingredients.

Arrange chicken legs in one layer in a shallow dish. Pour over the marinade, and gently shake chicken to coat. Let stand at room temperature for 2 hours, or cover and refrigerate overnight, turning pieces several times. If refrigerated, let chicken stand at room temperature for 30 minutes before cooking.

Light a fire in a charcoal grill. Wipe marinade from chicken and grill, turning occasionally, until golden on all sides and juices run clear when chicken is pierced, 20–30 minutes. Alternatively, cook chicken pieces under a broiler (grill). Lay chicken about 10 inches (25 cm) from the flame and cook, turning occasionally, until golden on all sides and juices run clear when chicken is pierced, 20–30 minutes.

Serves 4–6

Note: Traditionally, this dish is made with whole spatchcock chickens that have been butterflied, by splitting down the backbone and flattening. Broil (grill), skin-side down, for 10–15 minutes, then turn and broil, skin-side up, for 10 minutes. After cooking, cut chicken with a cleaver, through the bones, into smaller pieces. You may also use chicken halves.

Ingredients

FOR MARINADE

10 cloves garlic, coarsely chopped

3 stalks lemongrass, white part only, peeled and coarsely chopped

2 scallions (green onions), finely chopped

2 tablespoons fish sauce

2 tablespoons fresh lime juice

2 tablespoons dry white wine

½ cup (4 fl oz/125 ml) coconut milk

1 tablespoon Asian (toasted) sesame oil

½ teaspoon freshly ground black pepper

8 chicken legs

Ingredients

1 cup (2 oz/60 g) cloud or tree ear mushrooms (black or white fungus)

¼ cup (2 fl oz/60 ml) vegetable oil

6 cloves garlic, coarsely chopped

1 small onion, thinly sliced

12 oz (375 g) boneless, skinless chicken breasts, thinly sliced

1 cup (4 oz/125 g) loosely packed, julienned fresh ginger, preferably young ginger

1 tablespoon fish sauce

3 tablespoons oyster sauce

1 tablespoon soy sauce

1 tablespoon soybean paste

2 fresh long red chilies, cut into large pieces

½ cup (4 fl oz/125 ml) chicken broth or water

8 scallions (green onions), white part only, chopped

Chicken with ginger
Gai phad king

If using dried mushrooms, soak in water for 10 minutes; drain. Use scissors to trim hard core, then cut mushrooms into pieces.

Heat oil in a wok or large, heavy frying pan over high heat and fry garlic just until it starts to brown. Immediately add onion and chicken, and stir-fry until meat is opaque on all sides, about 2 minutes.

Add ginger and mushrooms, then fish sauce, oyster sauce, soy sauce, and soybean paste. Stir-fry for 1 minute. Add chilies and broth or water, bring to a boil, and cook for 1 minute. Stir in scallions.

Transfer to a serving dish and serve.

Serves 4–6

Note: If cloud or tree ear mushrooms are unavailable, substitute an equal quantity of straw mushrooms or standard mushrooms.

Beef with **basil leaves**

Phad krapow neua

Heat oil in a wok or large, heavy frying pan over high heat. Add garlic and chilies and stir-fry until garlic just begins to brown.

Add beef, stirring vigorously to break it up, about 2 minutes, then add oyster sauce, fish sauce, sweet soy sauce, and sugar to taste. Stir well to combine, then add chilies.

Add chicken broth or water and bring to boil. Add basil, cook for 1 minute, then remove from heat.

Transfer to a serving plate and serve.

Serves 4–6

Note: Traditionally, this dish is served for lunch.

Hint: For a less piquant dish, keep the chilies whole, or seed them.

Ingredients

3 tablespoons vegetable oil

15 cloves garlic, crushed

10 fresh red or green chilies, coarsely chopped

1 lb (500 g) ground (minced) beef

1 tablespoon oyster sauce

2 tablespoons fish sauce

1 teaspoon sweet (thick) soy sauce

1 tablespoon granulated (white) sugar (or to taste)

2 fresh long red chilies, cut into large pieces

1 cup (8 fl oz/250 ml) chicken broth or water

1½ cups (1½ oz/45 g) loosely packed fresh basil leaves, preferably holy basil

Ingredients

⅓ cup (3 fl oz/90 ml) vegetable oil

9 cloves garlic, crushed

1 lb (500 g) pumpkin or squash, peeled, seeded, and thinly sliced

½ cup (4 fl oz/125 ml) chicken broth or water

12 oz (375 g) boneless pork loin, cut into thin strips

¼ cup (2 fl oz/60 ml) fish sauce

2 eggs, lightly beaten

fresh sweet Thai basil leaves, for garnish

Pumpkin with **pork**

Phad fuk thong sai muu

Heat oil in a wok or large, heavy frying pan over medium-high heat. Add garlic, pumpkin or squash, and chicken broth or water. Bring to a boil.

Add pork, reduce heat, and simmer until meat is opaque throughout and pumpkin or squash is tender, about 5 minutes. Add fish sauce, then stir in eggs to just bind sauce.

Transfer to a serving dish, garnish with basil leaves and serve.

Serves 4–6

Hint
For a spectacular presentation, serve this dish in a hollowed-out pumpkin.

Ingredients

¼ cup (2 fl oz/60 ml) vegetable oil

2 Chinese sausages (gun chiang), cut in small rounds

2 tablespoons butter

½ teaspoon curry powder

3 cups (15 oz/470 g) cooked long-grain jasmine rice (see page 35)

1 small onion, coarsely chopped

3 scallions (green onions), chopped

1 firm tomato, coarsely chopped

½ cup (3 oz/90 g) raisins (sultanas)

½ cup (3 oz/90 g) coarsely chopped fresh pineapple pieces, or canned in water, and drained

1 teaspoon granulated (white) sugar

2 tablespoons soy sauce

Fried rice with **pineapple**

Khao op sapparot

Heat oil in a wok or large, heavy frying pan over medium-high heat and fry the sausages for 1 minute. Using a slotted spoon, transfer to paper towels to drain.

Add butter and curry powder to wok and fry, stirring constantly, until fragrant, about 1 minute. Stir in cooked rice until well coated. Add sausages, onion, scallions, tomato, raisins, and pineapple. Stir-fry for about 4 minutes, then add sugar and soy sauce.

Serves 4–6

Hint

For an impressive presentation, place a pineapple on its side on a cutting board and slice in half or slice off the top third lengthwise. Scoop the flesh from the bottom half or two-thirds to make a cavity. Set aside ½ cup (3 oz/90 g) pineapple for the recipe, and save the rest for another use. Spoon the fried rice into the hollowed-out pineapple, cover with the "lid," and serve.

Fried rice with lemongrass

Khao phad takrai

Heat oil in a wok or large, heavy frying pan over high heat. Add eggs and stir-fry until well cooked and dry, about 30 seconds. Add raw shrimp if using, and both varieties of sausages, and stir-fry for 1 minute.

Add rice and stir-fry until well mixed and heated through, about 2 minutes. Add lemongrass, soy sauce, sugar, and the cooked shrimp if using.

Stir to combine, and remove from heat. Sprinkle with basil and squeeze over fresh lime juice. Transfer to a platter and serve.

Serves 4–6

Hint

If desired, accompany this dish with shredded green mango, thinly sliced shallot, and sliced chilies.

Ingredients

¼ cup (2 fl oz/60 ml) vegetable oil

2 eggs, lightly beaten

⅓ cup (2 oz/60 g) shelled, raw or cooked shrimp (king prawns), coarsely diced

1 frankfurter, coarsely chopped

2 Chinese sausages (gun chiang), cut into thin rounds

4 cups (20 oz/625 g) cooked long-grain jasmine rice (see page 35)

4 stalks lemongrass, white part only, peeled and very finely chopped

¼ cup (2 fl oz/60 ml) light soy sauce

1 teaspoon granulated (white) sugar

½ cup (½ oz/15 g) loosely packed fresh sweet Thai basil leaves, torn

1 lime, quartered

Phad Thai noodles
Phad Thai

Soak noodles in cold water for about 10 minutes to soften; drain and set aside.

Heat oil in a wok or large, heavy frying pan over high heat. Add tofu, garlic, and dried shrimp and stir-fry until garlic begins to brown, about 1 minute. Add noodles and stir-fry carefully, so as not to break them. Add broth or water and continue cooking for 2–3 minutes, or until noodles are tender. Reduce heat to medium and add fish sauce, soy sauce, tamarind, and sugar. Cook until mixture sputters, then add eggs, and stir-fry constantly until eggs are cooked and dry, about 1–2 minutes. Add peanuts, chives, and bean sprouts, and stir to mix.

Transfer to a serving dish and serve, garnished with lime wedges.

Serves 4–6

Note: Phad Thai is a popular Thai dish found in all parts of the kingdom. The sen lek noodles used here are about the thickness of a bean sprout. You can substitute 14 oz (400 g) fresh rice noodles, but do not pre-soak.

Hint

For a striking presentation, fry a thin, flat omelette in a nonstick pan, and fold this over the fried-noodle mixture. Make a small incision at the top to expose the contents, and serve.

Ingredients

- 6 oz (180 g) dried rice noodles (sen lek)
- 3 tablespoons vegetable oil
- 3 oz (90 g) firm tofu, rinsed and patted dry, cut into small cubes
- 2 large cloves garlic, finely chopped
- 1 tablespoon dried shrimp
- ⅓ cup (3 fl oz/90 ml) chicken broth or water
- 3 tablespoons fish sauce
- 1 tablespoon soy sauce
- 1–2 tablespoons tamarind puree, to taste
- 2–3 tablespoons granulated (white) sugar, to taste
- 2 eggs, beaten
- 3 tablespoons chopped roasted peanuts
- 1 small bunch Chinese (garlic or flat) chives, or regular chives, cut into 1-inch (2.5-cm) pieces
- 1 cup (2 oz/60 g) bean sprouts
- 2 limes, cut into wedges

Ingredients

6 oz (180 g) cellophane
  (bean thread) noodles

¼ cup (2 fl oz/60 ml) vegetable oil

3 eggs, beaten

1 onion, cut into wedges

3 firm tomatoes, cut into
  4 or 8 wedges

3 cloves pickled garlic, coarsely
  chopped

2 tablespoons fish sauce

3 tablespoons oyster sauce

1 teaspoon granulated (white) sugar

½ teaspoon ground white pepper

2 scallions (green onions), finely
  chopped

Fried cellophane noodles
Phad wun sen

Soak noodles in cold water for at least 15 minutes, to soften. Drain and coarsely cut with scissors into 6-inch (15-cm) lengths.

Heat half the oil (2 tablespoons) in a wok or large, heavy frying pan over medium-high heat. Add eggs and stir-fry until cooked and dry, 1–2 minutes. Remove with a slotted spoon and reserve. Add remaining 2 tablespoons oil to the wok. Add noodles and stir-fry while adding onion, tomatoes, and pickled garlic. Stir-fry for 1 minute to heat through, then add fish sauce, oyster sauce, sugar, and white pepper and stir until well combined. Add 1½ scallions and eggs, stir to combine, and remove from heat.

Transfer to a serving dish, sprinkle with remaining half scallion and serve.

Serves 4–6

Hint:
If desired, noodles can be soaked several hours in advance, left in the water until ready to cook.

1

2

3

4

HOW TO MAKE CURRY BASES

Preparing your own coconut cream, coconut milk and curry paste guarantees freshness, and allows you to vary flavors to suit your taste, such as decreasing chili. However, commercial coconut milk, cream and curry pastes are perfectly suitable substitutes.

Step-by-Step making coconut **cream** and **milk**

1. Shake a whole dried coconut to hear the water inside. If there is none present, discard the coconut. Drill or nail holes in the eyes to release the water. Hold the coconut in your hand, rested in a heavy tea towel. Use a large chef's knife to crack the coconut by scoring lightly across its circumference, then striking it sharply with the back of the knife to crack the shell. Take extra care, lest you cut your hand. Alternatively, drop the coconut onto a hard concrete surface, or hit it with a hammer.

2. Use a small hand grater to scrape out the coconut meat in shreds. Alternatively, pry the meat from the shell, peel off the brown inner skin, and grate the meat in a food processor.

3. Put the grated coconut in a tea towel and wring it, or put it in a sieve and press it firmly with knuckles or the back of a large spoon, to extract the cream; reserve the liquid.

4. Add just enough warm or hot water to cover the shredded coconut and press it again to extract thick coconut milk; reserve. Repeat again, to extract thin coconut milk.

Step-by-Step grinding curry pastes

1

In a mortar and pestle

1. When making curry pastes, begin by toasting then grinding the dry spices (khong heng), while the inside of the mortar is still clean. Remove the powder (pong). Now, grind the other ingedients, starting with the hardest, most fibrous items and working down to the softer items. To facilitate pounding, coarsely cut the hardest ingredients, such as galangal and lemongrass, into slices or pieces. Softer ingredients like garlic and shallots can be added whole, as they mash easily.

2

2. Add the wet ingredients (khong sot). Pound all the wet ingredients to a paste in a stone mortar with a pestle. If using a pottery mortar and a wooden pestle, make the paste in 2 batches as you will not be able to grind as effectively—the crushed ingredients will create a "cushioned" barrier.

3. Add all the ground ingredients and pound to combine. The texture should be pastelike and relatively smooth.

3

4. Cover tightly and store in the refrigerator—curry pastes keep for 3–4 days. For longer preservation, fry the curry paste prior to storage. In a wok, heat about $^{1}/_{3}$ cup (3 fl oz/90 ml) oil. Or fry the paste over low heat, stirring occasionally, until aromatic and color changes slightly, 3–5 minutes. Store the chili paste in the cooking oil, and cover tightly. This will keep for up to 2 months in the refrigerator, and can be frozen indefinitely.

In a food processor

Coarsely chop all the fresh ingredients. Place the chopped ingredients and the spices in a food processor. Pulse on and off until even in texture, then process continuously to make a relatively smooth paste. If necessary, add a small amount of water, 1 teaspoon at a time, to facilitate the processing.

4

Step-by-Step basic coconut milk curry

1. In a wok or large saucepan over medium-high heat, bring the coconut cream or milk to a boil and cook, stirring constantly, until the oil begins to separate from the coconut. Note: Some canned coconut cream will not separate; if this occurs, add oil.

2. Add the curry paste all at once, stirring constantly, and cook until the aroma rises and the paste becomes fragrant, 1–2 minutes.

3. Add rich coconut milk, broth or water, plus longer-cooking ingredients such as meats on the bone or hard vegetables such as pumpkin or squash. Bring to a boil, then simmer, uncovered, until almost tender, 20–30 minutes. (If the meat in the recipe requires longer cooking, precook it separately.) Simmering coconut milk should not be covered, or it may curdle.

4. Add thin coconut milk, plus seasonings such as fish sauce and palm sugar, tough herbs such as kaffir lime leaf, and any remaining vegetables. Boil for a few minutes until tender.

5. Finally, add delicate greens or herbs such as basil and cilantro (fresh coriander). Remove from heat at once and garnish as directed. Note: If you are not ready to serve at this point, keep the curry in a warm place—off the heat—until ready to serve. Also, do not add the basil until the last minute, lest its flavor and texture become muddied.

Step-by-Step Northern curry

While coconut-milk based curries are common in Thailand's tropical south, the relative absence of coconut trees in the mountainous north make these less popular there. Unlike most southern curries, here the paste is fried in oil and not coconut cream, and the liquid is usually water or broth.

1. In a wok or large saucepan, heat oil over medium-high heat and add the curry paste. Fry, stirring constantly, until fragrant, 2–3 minutes.

2. Add broth or water and bring to a boil.

3. Add ingredients in the same order listed for basic coconut milk curry.

Note: Unlike Western cooking, where meat is often seared before adding to a slow stew, Thai cooks commonly boil meat for a short time. Slower-cooking meats such as stewing beef should be cubed and gently braised in a tightly covered pot with a minimal amount water or thin coconut milk for 1–2 hours, or until tender. When meat is marinated in curry paste, such as in Hanglay curry with pork (page 85), fry the meat and marinade together until fragrant. Then add additional liquid and proceed as above.

1

2

3

Ingredients

20 dried long red chilies, seeded

2 tablespoons coriander seeds

4 cardamom pods

1 teaspoon black peppercorns

1 teaspoon salt

½-inch (12-mm) piece fresh galangal, coarsely chopped

½ stalk lemongrass, white part only, peeled and chopped

2 teaspoons chopped kaffir lime zest

8 cilantro (fresh coriander) roots, or 2 tablespoons coarsely chopped stems

⅓ cup (2 oz/60 g) finely chopped shallots (French shallots), preferably pink

6 large cloves garlic, crushed

2 teaspoons dried shrimp paste

20 fresh small red chilies

Red curry paste
Nam prik gaeng phed

Soak dried chilies in warm water for about 10 minutes. In a small frying pan over medium heat, separately toast the coriander seeds, cardamom pods and peppercorns, stirring constantly, until fragrant. Immediately pour into a mortar. Add salt and grind together into a fine powder with a pestle. Transfer to a small bowl.

Add all remaining ingredients to the mortar, and pound to a paste, 10–20 minutes. Halfway through, drain the chilies, coarsely chop, then add them to the mortar and pound until well blended. Finally, stir in the ground spices. Or your can coarsely chop all the ingredients then put them in a food processor and process until finely chopped. If necessary, add a small amount of water, 1 teaspoon at a time (see also How to make curry bases, page 56).

Makes about 1 cup

Note: Although green curry is one of the most popular dishes in the West, red curry is more popular in Thailand because it is more versatile.

Making your own curry paste allows you to vary the ingredients to suit your taste: you can decrease the quantity of chilies or chili seeds, or increase the citrus flavors of kaffir lime, lemongrass, or cilantro, for example. Make more curry paste than you need, and store the remainder for future use. Tightly covered, fresh curry paste keeps for 3–4 days in the refrigerator, and fried curry paste keeps for up to two months in the refrigerator, or indefinitely in the freezer.

Suggested Menu

Fish cakes with sweet chili relish; Spicy cellophane noodle salad; Jungle curry with pork; Chicken with ginger; and Fried rice with lemongrass.

Jungle curry with pork

Gaeng pah muu

Heat oil in a wok or large, heavy frying pan over medium-high heat. Add curry paste and fry, stirring constantly, for 1–2 minutes. Add pork and stir-fry until it changes color on all sides, about 2 minutes.

Add eggplants, beans, krachai, peppercorns, corn and 1 cup (8 fl oz/250 ml) broth or water. Bring to a boil, stirring often, then simmer, uncovered, for 2 minutes. Add the remaining broth, increase heat and bring to a boil.

Tear kaffir lime leaves and basil into pieces. Stir lime leaves, salt, fish sauce, and chili into the curry. Boil for 1 minute. Add basil leaves and immediately remove from heat. Transfer to a serving dish, and serve.

Serves 4–6

Variation

Replace pork with an equal quantity of beef or chicken. Traditionally, wild boar is used in this recipe.

Ingredients

- ¼ cup (2 fl oz/60 ml) vegetable oil
- ¼ cup (2 fl oz/60 ml) fresh or commercial Red curry paste (see page 60)
- 12 oz (375 g) boneless pork butt or loin, thinly sliced
- ¼ cup (1 oz/30 g) chopped eggplant (aubergine)
- ¼ cup (1 oz/30 g) pea eggplants (optional)
- 2 long beans or 8 green beans, cut into 1-inch (2.5-cm) pieces
- ½ cup (2 oz/60 g) julienned krachai (Chinese keys)
- ¼ cup fresh green peppercorns on stem, or 1–2 tablespoons canned green peppercorns, drained
- 6 ears fresh or canned baby corn, rinsed and drained, cut into large pieces
- 2 cups (16 fl oz/500 ml) chicken broth or water
- 5 kaffir lime leaves, stemmed
- ½ cup (½ oz/15 g) loosely packed fresh Thai basil leaves, preferably holy basil
- ¼ teaspoon salt
- 2 tablespoons fish sauce
- 1 fresh long red chili, cut into large pieces

Ingredients

about 2 cups (16 fl oz/500 ml) coconut milk

2–3 tablespoons vegetable oil

¼ cup (2 fl oz/60 ml) fresh or commercial Red curry paste (page 60)

½ cup (2 oz/60 g) chopped round Thai or purple eggplant (aubergine)

1 cup (3½ oz/100 g) coarsely chopped fresh or canned bamboo shoots, rinsed and drained

3 kaffir lime leaves, stemmed

1 cup (1 oz/30 g) loosely packed fresh sweet Thai basil leaves

1–2 tablespoons fish sauce, to taste

12 oz (375 g) fish fillets such as snapper, bream, or perch, thinly sliced

2 fresh long red chilies, cut into large pieces

Red curry with **fish**
Gaeng phed plaa

Let coconut milk stand until the thick coconut milk rises to the top. Spoon the thick coconut milk into a bowl, reserving 2 tablespoons for garnish. Heat oil in a wok or large frying pan over medium-high heat and fry the curry paste, stirring constantly, until fragrant, 1–2 minutes. Add the thick coconut milk, stir to combine, and bring to a boil. Add eggplant, bamboo shoots and remaining thin coconut milk. Reduce heat and simmer, uncovered, until vegetables are slightly soft, about 4 minutes.

Tear 2 kaffir lime leaves and basil into pieces. Stir fish sauce and lime leaves into curry. Add fish and cook for about 2 minutes, or until fish flakes when prodded. Add half the basil leaves and remove from heat.

Transfer curry to a serving dish and garnish with remaining basil. Drizzle with 2 tablespoons of reserved thick coconut milk. Roll the remaining lime leaf into a tight cylinder and cut into fine strips; sprinkle over curry.

Serves 4–6

Note: Most varieties of fish fillet will suit here, but don't stir too vigorously, or the pieces may break up. Firm-textured fish, such as cod or even sturgeon, hold up best, but may require longer cooking time.

Variation

Red curry with lobster (Gaeng phed kung mangkawn)

Remove meat from the shells of 2 rock lobster tails and cut into pieces. Heat ¼ cup (2 fl oz/60 ml) vegetable oil in a wok or frying pan over high heat and stir-fry lobster meat for 3–4 minutes, or until opaque throughout. Using a slotted spoon, transfer to a bowl. Proceed as above, omitting fish. Just before serving, return lobster meat to the curry to heat through. Garnish and serve.

Red curry with roast duck

Gaeng Phed Ped Yang

Bone and skin duck. Let coconut milk stand, allowing the thick coconut milk to rise to the top. Spoon thick coconut milk into a small bowl, reserving 2 tablespoons for garnish.

In a wok or large, heavy frying pan over medium-high heat, fry the thick coconut milk, stirring constantly, until it begins to separate, 3–5 minutes. If it does not separate, add the optional oil. Add red curry paste and fry, stirring constantly, until fragrant, 1–2 minutes. Tear 2 kaffir lime leaves and basil into pieces.

Add remaining thin coconut milk to the wok, increase heat, and bring to a gentle boil. Add duck and simmer until heated through, about 5 minutes. Add torn lime leaves, green peppercorns, both varieties of eggplants, pineapple and cherry tomatoes. Reduce heat and simmer for 3 minutes. Add water, if necessary. Add all remaining ingredients, reserving a few basil leaves and the remaining kaffir lime leaf for garnish.

Transfer to a serving bowl, garnish with reserved basil, and drizzle with reserved thick coconut milk. Roll the remaining kaffir lime leaf into a tight cylinder and cut into fine shreds; sprinkle over curry.

Serves 4–6

Hint
Roasted ducks are readily available in Chinese delicatessans and at numerous Asian markets.

Ingredients

roast duck (page 36), or about 12 oz (375 g) roasted, boneless duck meat

2 cups (16 fl oz/500 ml) coconut milk

2–3 tablespoons vegetable oil (optional)

3 tablespoons fresh or commercial Red curry paste (page 60)

3 kaffir limes leaves, stemmed

1 cup (1 oz/30 g) loosely packed fresh sweet Thai basil leaves

½ cup (2 oz/40 g) fresh green peppercorns on the stem, or 2–4 tablespoons canned green peppercorns, drained

1 cup (4 oz/125 g) eggplant (aubergine) cut into ½-inch (12-mm) pieces or 4 round Thai eggplants

½ cup (2 oz/60 g) pea eggplants (optional)

1 cup (6 oz/185 g) fresh or canned pineapple chunks, drained

6 cherry tomatoes

10 grapes

1 fresh long red chili, coarsely chopped

2 tablespoons fish sauce

2 tablespoons soy sauce

1 tablespoon granulated (white) sugar

1 tablespoon palm sugar

Ingredients

1 lb (500 g) fish fillets, such as red fish, cod, monkfish, trout, or salmon, skinned

10 kaffir lime leaves, stemmed

1 tablespoon palm sugar

⅓ cup (3 fl oz/90 ml) fresh or commercial Red curry paste (page 60)

1 tablespoon fish sauce

1 egg, beaten

½ cup (2 oz/60 g) tapioca starch

2 teaspoons baking powder

8 long beans, or about 30 green beans, cut into very thin rounds

vegetable oil for deep-frying

Sweet chili relish (page 121) for serving

Fish cakes
Tord man plaa

In a food processor, pulse fish until finely ground. Roll kaffir lime leaves into a tight cylinder and cut into fine shreds; add to the food processor. Add the sugar, red curry paste, fish sauce, egg, and baking powder and process until just blended, no more than 5 seconds. Transfer to a bowl and stir in beans. Cover and keep in the refrigerator for up to 1 day.

To cook, in a wok or deep-fryer, heat 3 inches (7.5 cm) oil to 325°F (170°C). Lightly moisten your fingertips to prevent sticking, and form a walnut-sized portion of fish paste into a small patty about 2 inches (5 cm) in diameter, and ¼ inch (6 mm) thick. Carefully add a few fish cakes at a time to the oil and cook until golden brown and well puffed, 2–3 minutes. Using a skimmer, transfer to paper towels to drain. Serve hot, accompanied with sweet chili relish.

Makes about 25 cakes

Note: Fish cakes freeze extremely well after cooking. To reheat, first defrost overnight in the refrigerator, then reheat in a preheated 350°F(180°C) oven until heated through, 15–20 minutes.

Variation
The fish here can be substituted with 1 lb (500 g) boneless, skinless chicken, pork, or raw (green) shrimp (prawns).

Ingredients

1¼ cups (10 fl oz/300 ml) vegetable oil

¼ cup (2 fl oz/60 ml) fresh or commercial Red curry paste (page 60)

1 cup (8 fl oz/250 ml) coconut cream, plus 2 tablespoons, for garnish

12 oz (375 g) beef round, blade, or sirloin, trimmed and cut into very thin strips

1 cup (3½ oz/100 g) chopped eggplant (aubergine) or 3 round Thai eggplants, quartered then sliced

1 cup (4 oz/125 g) pea eggplants (optional)

¼ cup fresh green peppercorns on stems, or 2 tablespoons canned peppercorns, drained

6 kaffir lime leaves, stemmed

1 cup (4 oz/125 g) julienned krachai (Chinese keys)

2 tablespoons fish sauce

1 tablespoon soy sauce

1 teaspoon granulated (white) sugar

¼ cup (2 fl oz/60 ml) chicken broth or water

1 fresh long red chili, coarsely chopped

1 cup (1 oz/30 g) loosely packed fresh sweet Thai basil leaves

Stir-fried beef with **red curry paste**

Phad phet neua

Heat ¼ cup (2 fl oz/60 ml) oil in a wok or large, heavy frying pan over medium-high heat. Add curry paste and fry, stirring constantly, until fragrant, 1–2 minutes. Add ½ cup (4 fl oz/125 ml) coconut cream, and beef. Stir until gently boiling. Cook 2 minutes for sirloin, or up to 30 minutes for tougher cuts like blade.

Add eggplants and peppercorns. Add kaffir lime leaves and krachai and cook, stirring, for 1 minute. Add fish sauce, soy sauce, sugar, and broth or water. Boil for 1 minute. Stir in the remaining ½ cup (4 fl oz/125 ml) coconut cream and chili. Remove from heat. Wash and pat the basil leaves completely dry with paper towels.

Heat remaining 1 cup (8 fl oz/250 ml) oil in a wok until surface shimmers. Add basil leaves all at once and fry for a few seconds, or until lightly crisp. To serve, transfer beef mixture to a platter, and top with fried basil. Drizzle with reserved 2 tablespoons coconut cream.

Serves 4

Long beans with **pork** and **red** curry paste

Phad phed tua sai muu

Heat oil in a wok or large, heavy skillet over medium-high heat. Add curry paste and cook, stirring constantly, until fragrant, 1–2 minutes. Add meat and stir until opaque on all sides, 2–3 minutes. Add 10 kaffir lime leaves, beans, and chilies. Cook, stirring frequently, for about 2 minutes, or until meat is barely tender.

Add palm sugar—if using a wok, add it along the edge of the wok so that it melts before stirring into the other ingredients; if using a standard saucepan, add directly to the pan. Add granulated sugar, then fish sauce and basil. Stir well, then remove from heat and transfer to a platter.

Roll remaining kaffir lime leaves into a tight cylinder and cut into fine shreds. Sprinkle over the dish and serve.

Serves 4

Ingredients

¼ cup (2 fl oz/60 ml) vegetable oil

1 cup (8 fl oz/250 ml) fresh or commercial Red curry paste (page 60)

20 oz (625 g) boneless pork butt or loin, thinly sliced

15 kaffir lime leaves, stemmed

1 lb (500 g) long beans or green beans, cut into 1-inch (2.5-cm) pieces

5 fresh long red chilies, seeded and cut into strips

1 tablespoon palm sugar

2 tablespoons granulated (white) sugar

¼ cup (2 fl oz/60 ml) fish sauce

1 cup (1 oz/30 g) loosely packed fresh sweet Thai basil leaves, coarsely torn

Green curry paste

Nam prik gaeng kheo wan

Ingredients

2 teaspoons coriander seeds

1 teaspoon cumin seeds

1 teaspoon black peppercorns

1 teaspoon salt

6 thin slices fresh galangal, chopped

2 stalks lemongrass, white part only, peeled and chopped

2 teaspoons chopped kaffir lime zest

about 15 cilantro (fresh coriander) roots, or ¼ cup (1 oz/30 g) coarsely chopped stems

¼ cup (1 oz/30 g) finely chopped shallots (French shallots), preferably pink

2 large cloves garlic, crushed

2 teaspoons dried shrimp paste

2 teaspoons coarsely chopped, peeled fresh turmeric or 1 teaspoon ground turmeric

40 fresh small green chilies

2 cups (2 oz/60 g) loosely packed fresh sweet Thai basil leaves

In a small dry skillet or frying pan over medium heat, separately toast each spice, stirring constantly, until fragrant, no more than 90 seconds. Immediately pour into a mortar or spice grinder. Add salt and grind to a fine powder; reserve.

Put all remaining ingredients in a large mortar and pound with a pestle until pulverized, 10–20 minutes. Stir in reserved spices. Or, coarsely chop all ingredients then process in a food processor until pulverized. If necessary, add a small amount of water, 1 teaspoon at a time (see also How to make curry bases, page 56).

Makes about 1 cup

Hint

For a less spicy curry paste, slice the chilies lengthwise and scrape away the seeds. Make more curry paste than you need, and store the remainder for future use. Tightly covered, fresh curry paste keeps for 3–4 days in the refrigerator. Fried curry paste keeps for 2 months in the refrigerator, or indefinitely in the freezer.

Note

Making your own curry paste allows you to vary the ingredients to suit your taste: you can decrease the quantity of chilies or chili seeds, for example.

Suggested menu

Tom yam soup; Green curry with chicken; Fish with green curry paste; Stir-fried beef with basil leaves; Fish sauce with chilies; and steamed rice.

Fish with green curry paste

Phad kheo wan plaa

Ingredients

¼ cup (2 fl oz/60 ml) vegetable oil

¼ cup (2 fl oz/60 ml) fresh or commercial Green curry paste (page 70)

12 oz (375 g) white fish fillets such as snapper, sole, or cod, thinly sliced

4 kaffir lime leaves, stemmed

1 cup (4 oz/125 g) chopped eggplant (aubergine) or 3 round Thai eggplants, chopped

½ cup (2 oz/60 g) pea eggplants (optional)

¼ cup (2 fl oz/60 ml) fish broth or water

1 fresh long red chili, coarsely chopped

1 cup (1 oz/30 g) loosely packed fresh sweet Thai basil leaves

⅓ cup (3 fl oz/90 ml) coconut cream plus 2 tablespoons, for garnish

1 tablespoon fish sauce

1 tablespoon soy sauce

1 tablespoon granulated (white) sugar

1 tablespoon palm sugar

In a wok or large, heavy frying pan, heat oil over medium-high heat. Add curry paste and fry, stirring constantly, until fragrant, 1–2 minutes. Add fish and gently stir until coated on all sides. Add kaffir lime leaves and eggplants. Cook for 1 minute, then add broth or water.

Bring just to a boil, stirring, then add chili, basil, ⅓ cup (3 fl oz/90 ml) coconut cream, fish sauce, soy sauce and sugars. Cook for 1–2 minutes to heat through. Transfer to a serving bowl, drizzle over the remaining 2 tablespoons coconut cream, and serve.

Note: This is delicious chilled as well as hot but when serving chilled, delete the coconut cream garnish.

Variation

Pork with green curry paste (Phad kheo wan moo)
Substitute an equal quantity pork shoulder, loin, or tenderloin for the fish. Slice thinly, and proceed as above. Lamb leg or loin also makes a delicious substitute here, although it is not traditionally Thai.

Ingredients

2 cups (16 fl oz/500 ml) coconut milk

1–2 tablespoons vegetable oil (optional)

¼ cup (2 fl oz/60 ml) fresh or commercial Green curry paste (page 70)

12 oz (375 g) boneless, skinless chicken breasts, thinly sliced

½ cup (2 oz/60 g) chopped eggplant (aubergine) or 3 round Thai eggplants

¼ cup (1 oz/30 g) pea eggplants (optional)

2 tablespoons palm sugar (optional)

2 kaffir lime leaves, stemmed

½ cup (½ oz/15 g) loosely packed fresh sweet Thai basil leaves

2 tablespoons fish sauce

1 fresh long green chili, cut into large pieces

1 fresh long red chili, cut into large pieces

Green curry with chicken

Gaeng kheo wan gai

Let coconut milk stand, allowing the thick coconut milk to rise to the top. Spoon thick coconut milk into a small bowl, and reserve 2 tablespoons of this for garnish.

In a wok or large, heavy frying pan, heat thick coconut milk over medium-high heat for 3–5 minutes, stirring constantly, until it separates. If it does not separate, add optional oil. Add green curry paste and fry, stirring constantly, until fragrant, about 2 minutes.

Add chicken and cook until meat is opaque on all sides, 2–3 minutes. Add remaining thin coconut milk and bring to a boil. Add both the eggplants and simmer for 4 minutes, or until slightly soft. If desired, add palm sugar to taste. Tear kaffir lime leaves and basil into pieces. Stir in fish sauce, lime leaves and half of the basil.

Remove from heat and transfer to a serving bowl. Drizzle over reserved 2 tablespoons coconut cream. Garnish with green and red chilies and remaining basil leaves, and serve.

Serves 4–6

Variation

To make green curry with shrimp (gaeng kheo wan goong), substitute an equal amount of shelled and deveined jumbo shrimp (king prawns), with tails attached. Add raw shrimp soon after the eggplants and cook briskly for 2 minutes. If using raw shrimp, make sure the liquid is boiling when adding them, lest they turn mushy. Cooked shrimp should be added only during final minute of cooking to heat through.

Vegetarian green curry

Gaeng kheo wan jaay

Pat tofu dry with a paper towel. Heat oil in a large frying pan and working in batches, fry tofu cubes until golden. Remove using a slotted spoon and drain on paper towels; reserve.

Let coconut milk stand, allowing the thick coconut milk to rise to the top. Spoon thick coconut milk into a small bowl, reserving 2 tablespoons for garnish.

In a wok or large, heavy frying pan, heat thick coconut milk over medium-high heat for 3–5 minutes, stirring constantly, until it separates. If it does not separate, add optional oil. Add green curry paste and fry, stirring constantly, until fragrant, 1–2 minutes. Add vegetables and fried tofu and stir until well coated. Add remaining thin coconut milk and bring to a boil. Reduce heat and simmer until vegetables are slightly soft, about 4 minutes.

Add palm sugar—if using a wok, add it along the edge of the wok so that it melts before stirring into the curry; if using a standard frying pan, add directly to the curry. Tear kaffir lime leaves and basil into pieces. Stir in soy sauce, kaffir lime leaves and half the basil.

Remove from heat and transfer to a serving bowl. Drizzle over reserved 2 tablespoons thick coconut milk. Garnish with green and red chilies, and remaining basil leaves and serve.

Serves 4

Ingredients

- 5 oz (150 g) firm tofu, drained then cut into 3/4-inch (2-cm) cubes
- 1 cup (8 fl oz/250 ml) vegetable oil
- 2 cups (16 fl oz/500 ml) coconut milk
- 1–2 tablespoons vegetable oil (optional)
- 1/4 cup (2 fl oz/60 ml) fresh or commercial Green curry paste (page 70)
- 1/2 cup (2 oz/60 g) chopped eggplant (aubergine) or 3 round Thai eggplants, chopped
- 1/2 cup (2 oz/60 g) pea eggplants (optional)
- 1 cup (4 oz/125 g) coarsely chopped fresh or canned bamboo shoots, rinsed and drained
- 6 ears fresh or canned baby corn, rinsed and drained, cut into bite-sized pieces
- 2 tablespoons palm sugar
- 2 kaffir lime leaves, stemmed
- 1 cup (1 oz/30 g) loosely packed fresh sweet Thai basil leaves
- 2 tablespoons soy sauce
- 1 fresh long green chili, cut into large pieces
- 1 fresh long red chili, cut into large pieces

Ingredients

25 dried long red chilies, seeded

1 teaspoon salt

1-inch (2.5-cm) piece galangal, coarsely chopped

2 teaspoons coarsely chopped fresh turmeric, or 1 teaspoon ground turmeric

2 stalks lemongrass, white part only, peeled and chopped

8 large cloves garlic, crushed

2 teaspoons dried shrimp paste

Yellow curry paste
Nam prik gaeng garee

Soak dried chilies in warm water for 10 minutes. In a mortar, combine all remaining ingredients and pound to a paste with a pestle, 10–20 minutes. Halfway through, drain chilies, coarsely chop, and add to mortar. Or, coarsely chop all ingredients and put in a food processor. Process to a smooth paste. If necessary, add a small amount of water, 1 teaspoon at a time.

Makes about 1 cup (8 fl oz/250 ml)

Note

Commercial yellow curry paste is not as commonly available as red or green curry paste. Making your own curry paste allows you to vary the ingredients to suit your taste: you can decrease the quantity of chilies or chili seeds, for example.

Hint

Make more curry paste than you need, and store the remainder for future use. Tightly covered, fresh curry paste keeps for 3–4 days in the refrigerator. Fried curry paste keeps for two months in the refrigerator, or indefinitely in the freezer. (See also How to make curry bases, page 56.)

Suggested Menu

Spicy cellophane noodle salad; Yellow curry with chicken and Adjat sauce; Soybean dipping sauce; Fried fish with chili and basil; and Fried rice with pineapple.

Yellow curry with chicken

Gaeng garee gai

Ingredients

- 2 medium potatoes, peeled and cut into ¹⁄₂-inch (12-mm) pieces
- 2 cups (16 fl oz/500 ml) coconut milk
- 2–3 tablespoons vegetable oil (optional)
- ¹⁄₄ cup (2 fl oz/60 ml) fresh or commercial Yellow curry paste (page 76)
- 1 teaspoon curry powder
- 12 oz (375 g) boneless, skinless chicken breasts, thinly sliced
- 2 tablespoons palm sugar
- 2–3 tablespoons soy sauce, to taste
- Adjat sauce for serving (page 121)

Cook potatoes in a saucepan of salted boiling water until barely tender, 3–5 minutes; drain and set aside.

Let coconut milk stand, allowing the thick coconut milk to rise to the top. Spoon thick coconut milk into a small bowl, and reserve 2 tablespoons for garnish.

In a wok or large, heavy frying pan, heat thick coconut milk over medium-high heat for 3–5 minutes, stirring constantly, until it separates. If it does not separate, add optional oil. Add curry paste and curry powder and fry, stirring constantly, until fragrant, 1–2 minutes. Add chicken and potatoes, stirring gently to coat well.

Add remaining thin coconut milk and bring to a boil. Add palm sugar— if using a wok, add it along the edge of the wok so that it melts before stirring into the curry; if using a standard frying pan, add directly to the curry. Add soy sauce to taste, and simmer for 5 minutes. Transfer to a serving bowl. Accompany with adjat sauce.

Serves 4–6

Variations

1. Yellow curry with chicken drumsticks

Add 6 chicken legs to the fried curry paste. Stir in thin coconut milk, bring to a gentle boil, and cook, uncovered, until chicken juices run clear when pierced with a knife, 20–30 minutes. Add parboiled potatoes, cook another 5 minutes before serving.

2. Vegetarian yellow curry (Gaeng garee jaay)

Substitute 1 large carrot, peeled and cubed; 1 sweet potato, peeled and cubed; and ¹⁄₃ cup (2 oz/60 g) peeled and cubed pumpkin for chicken. Cook vegetables in salted boiling water until just tender, about 5 minutes. Drain and proceed as above adding vegetables with potatoes.

Ingredients

8 dried long red chilies, seeded

¼ cup (20 g) coriander seeds

2 tablespoons cumin seeds

4 star anise pods, crushed

2 cinnamon quills, broken

10 cloves

1 teaspoon salt

⅔ cup (5 fl oz/150 ml) vegetable oil

6 large cloves garlic, crushed

2 tablespoons finely chopped shallots (French shallots), preferably pink

6 thin slices galangal, chopped

1 stalk lemongrass, white part only, peeled and chopped

1 teaspoon chopped kaffir lime zest

Massaman curry paste
Nam prik gaeng massaman

Soak dried chilies in warm water for 10 minutes. Drain and pat dry. In a small frying pan over medium heat, separately toast each spice, stirring constantly, until fragrant. Immediately remove from heat and pour spices into a large mortar or spice grinder. Add salt and grind to a fine powder. Transfer to a small bowl.

Heat oil in a wok or large, heavy frying pan over medium-high heat. Add the garlic, shallots, and drained chilies. Fry until slightly golden, 1–2 minutes. Remove with a slotted spoon, reserve solids and discard oil. Add galangal, lemongrass, and kaffir lime zest to a large mortar, and pound to a paste, 10–20 minutes. Halfway through, add fried garlic, shallots, and chilies and pound until smooth. Add ground spices. Alternatively, grind dried spices then coarsely chop fresh ingredients, and place them in a food processor and process until finely chopped. If necessary, add a small amount of water, 1 teaspoon at a time. (See also How to make curry bases, page 56.)

Makes about ¾ cup (6 fl oz/180 ml)

Note: Making your own curry paste allows you to vary the ingredients to suit your taste. Tightly covered, fresh curry paste keeps for 3–4 days in the refrigerator. Fried curry paste keeps for two months in the refrigerator, or indefinitely in the freezer.

Suggested Menu

Tom yam soup with chicken; Massaman curry with lamb or beef and Adjat sauce; Crab with yellow curry powder; Phad Thai noodles; Fish sauce with chilies; and steamed rice.

Massaman curry with lamb

Gaeng massaman ghe

Let coconut milk stand, allowing the thick coconut milk to rise to the top. Spoon the thick coconut milk into a small bowl, and reserve 2 tablespoons for garnish.

In a wok or large, heavy frying pan, heat the thick coconut milk over medium-high heat for 3–5 minutes, stirring constantly, until it separates. If it does not separate, add optional oil. Add curry paste and fry, stirring constantly, until fragrant, 1–2 minutes.

Add meat and potatoes or other vegetable, and cook until lamb is lightly browned on both sides, 2–3 minutes. Add remaining thin coconut milk, increase heat, and bring to a boil. Add palm sugar—if using a wok, add it along the edge of the wok so that it melts before stirring into the curry; if using a standard frying pan, add directly to the curry. Add remaining ingredients and bring just to a boil.

Reduce heat and simmer until vegetables are tender, about 20 minutes. Transfer to a serving bowl, and serve with adjat sauce.

Serves 4–6

Note: Massaman curry is named after Thailand's Moslem minority living in the south, and is consequently never made with pork. It is popular throughout the kingdom.

Variation

Massaman curry with beef (Gaeng massaman neua)
Substitute an equal amount of cubed beef chuck, round (topside), or blade steak for the lamb. Tougher meat cuts may require thinner slicing and longer simmering (see also How to make curry bases, pages 58–59).

Ingredients

2 cups (16 fl oz/500 ml) coconut milk

2–3 tablespoons vegetable oil (optional)

¼ cup (2 fl oz/60 ml) fresh or commercial Massaman curry paste (page 78)

12 oz (375 g) boneless lamb leg, thinly sliced

2 potatoes, or 12 oz (375 g) sweet potato, taro, or pumpkin, peeled and cubed

1 teaspoon palm sugar

5 bay leaves

5 cardamom pods, toasted

2–3 tablespoons fish sauce

3–5 tablespoons tamarind puree, to taste

Adjat Sauce (page 121) for serving

Ingredients

25 dried long red chilies

1 tablespoon coriander seeds

1 teaspoon cumin seeds

6 blades mace, or 2 teaspoons ground mace

4 cardamom pods

2 teaspoons black peppercorns

1 teaspoon salt

1-inch (2.5-cm) piece fresh galangal, coarsely chopped

1 stalk lemongrass, white part only, peeled and chopped

2 teaspoons chopped kaffir lime zest

8 cilantro (fresh coriander) roots, or 2 tablespoons chopped stems

1/3 cup (2 oz/60 g) chopped shallots (French shallots), preferably pink

4 large cloves garlic, crushed

2 teaspoons dried shrimp paste

PENANG CURRY RECIPES

"Penang" does not refer to the Malaysian island Penang. "Penang" is the English transliteration of the Thai curry "phanaeng," or "panaeng." Despite the similar name, this curry belies its origin. There is, however, a slight similarity in the pronunciation.

Penang curry paste
Nam prik Panaeng

Soak dried chilies in warm water for 10 minutes. In a small dry frying pan over medium heat, separately toast each spice, stirring constantly, until fragrant. Immediately pour spices into a large mortar or spice grinder. Add salt and pound or grind to a fine powder. Transfer to a small bowl.

Add all remaining ingredients to a large mortar, and pound to a paste, 10–20 minutes. Halfway through, drain the chilies, coarsely chop, then add them to the mortar and pound until well blended. Stir in ground spices. Or, coarsely chop all fresh (or wet) ingredients, then put them in a food processor with the ground spices and process to a paste. If necessary, add a small amount of water, 1 teaspoon at a time. (See also How to make curry bases, page 56.)

Makes about 2/3 cup (5 fl oz/150 ml)

Note: 1. Penang is the only Thai curry not called "gaeng." In Asia, and some specialist shops, you may be able to get long pepper (phrik haang), a derivative of peppercorns. If available, add 3 long peppers, preferably fresh or green, and decrease the black pepper to 1/2 teaspoon. 2. Making your own curry paste allows you to vary the ingredients to suit your taste, such as decreasing the quantity of chilies or chili seeds.

Suggested Menu

Beef salad; Fried cellophane noodles; Penang curry with pork; Fried fish with Penang curry sauce; and steamed rice.

Penang curry with pork

Panaeng muu

Ingredients

- 2 cups (16 fl oz/500 ml) coconut cream plus 2 tablespoons for garnish
- 2–3 tablespoons vegetable oil (optional)
- 1/4 cup (2 fl oz/60 ml) Penang curry paste (see page 80) or fresh or commercial Red curry paste (page 60)
- 12 oz (375 g) pork tenderloin, thinly sliced
- 2 tablespoons palm sugar
- 2–3 tablespoons fish sauce, to taste
- 7 kaffir lime leaves, stemmed
- 1/2 cup (1/2 oz/15 g) loosely packed fresh sweet Thai basil leaves
- 1 fresh long red chili, cut into thin strips

In a wok or large, heavy frying pan over medium-high heat, cook 1 cup (8 fl oz/250 ml) coconut cream, stirring constantly, until it separates, 3–5 minutes. If it does not separate, add the optional oil. Add the curry paste and fry, stirring constantly, until fragrant, 1–2 minutes.

Add pork, and stir until meat is opaque on both sides, about 2 minutes. Add remaining 1 cup (8 fl oz/250 ml) coconut cream and bring to a boil. Add palm sugar—if using a wok, add it along the edge of the wok so that it melts before stirring into the curry; if using a standard frying pan, add directly to the curry. Stir in fish sauce to taste, and simmer until meat is tender, about 3 minutes.

Roll 4 kaffir lime leaves into a tight cylinder and cut into fine shreds; set aside. Tear remaining 3 kaffir lime leaves and basil into pieces. Add torn lime leaves and half the basil to curry. Stir to combine. Transfer to a serving dish.

Drizzle with 2 tablespoons coconut cream. Garnish with shredded lime leaves, chili, and remaining basil.

Serves 4–6

Note: Tougher cuts of meat require longer cooking, 15–30 minutes. If using, do not add sugar and remaining ingredients until after meat is tender, then proceed as directed.

Variation

Penang curry with pumpkin (Panaeng fuk-tong)

Substitute 2 cups thinly sliced and peeled pumpkin or butternut squash for pork. Substitute soy sauce for fish sauce and cook as above, or until tender.

Ingredients

12 oz (375 g) fish fillets such as snapper, plaice, or halibut, thinly sliced

1 cup (5 oz/150 g) all-purpose (plain) flour, for dredging

vegetable oil for deep-frying

2 cups (16 fl oz/500 ml) coconut cream plus 3 tablespoons for garnish

2–3 tablespoons vegetable oil (optional)

¼ cup (2 fl oz/60 ml) Penang curry paste (page 80) or fresh or commercial Red curry paste (page 60)

2 tablespoons palm sugar

2 tablespoons fish sauce

6 kaffir lime leaves, stemmed

½ cup (½ oz/15 g) loosely packed fresh sweet Thai basil leaves

1 fresh long red chili, seeded and julienned

Fried fish with **Penang curry sauce**
Choo chee plaa

Pat fish pieces dry with paper towels, then dredge in flour to coat evenly. Shake off any excess flour and set aside.

In a wok or deep-fryer, heat 3 inches (7.5 cm) oil to 350°F (180°C). Fry fish in batches until golden brown, about 3 minutes. Using a skimmer, transfer fish to paper towels to drain briefly. Place in a deep serving dish.

In a wok or large, heavy frying pan over medium-high heat, fry 1 cup (8 fl oz/250 ml) coconut cream, stirring constantly, until it separates, 3–5 minutes. If it does not separate, add the optional oil. Add the curry paste and fry, stirring constantly, until fragrant, 1–2 minutes. Add remaining 1 cup (8 fl oz/250 ml) coconut cream and stir-fry for 1 minute. Add palm sugar—if using a wok, add it along the edge of the wok so that it melts before stirring into the curry; if using a standard frying pan, add directly to the curry. Stir in fish sauce to taste.

Roll lime leaves into a tight cylinder and cut into fine shreds. Tear basil leaves coarsely into pieces. Add half the lime leaves, basil, and chili to the curry. Stir to combine then pour over fish in serving dish.

Garnish with remaining lime leaves, chili, and remaining basil. Drizzle with reserved coconut cream, and serve.

Serves 4–6

Ingredients

6 dried long red chilies

1 teaspoon salt

2-inch (5-cm) piece galangal, coarsely chopped

1 stalk lemongrass, white part only, peeled and chopped

¼ cup chopped shallots (French shallots), preferably pink

2 large cloves garlic, crushed

2 teaspoons dried shrimp paste

2 teaspoons coarsely chopped fresh turmeric, or 1 teaspoon ground turmeric

Hanglay curry paste
Nam prik gaeng Hanglay

Soak dried chilies in warm water for 10 minutes. Meanwhile, combine all remaining ingredients in a large mortar, and pound to a paste with a pestle, 10–20 minutes. Halfway through, drain the chilies, coarsely chop, then add them to the mortar and pound until well blended. Or, coarsely chop all ingredients, then put them in a food processor and process until finely chopped. If necessary, add a small amount of water, 1 teaspoon at a time. (See also How to make curry bases, page 56.)

Makes about ¾ cup (6 fl oz/180 ml)

Note: Hanglay curry is a northern dish with influences from neighboring Burma.

Making your own curry paste allows you to vary the ingredients to suit your taste: you can decrease the quantity of chilies or chili seeds, for example.

Hint
Make more curry paste than you need, and store the remainder for future use. Tightly covered, fresh curry paste keeps for 3–4 days in the refrigerator. Fried curry paste keeps for two months in the refrigerator, or indefinitely in the freezer.

Suggested Menu
Green papaya salad; Larb chicken salad; Hanglay curry with pork; Gai yang chicken; Fish sauce with chilies; and sticky rice.

Hanglay curry with pork

Gaeng Hanglay muu

In a large bowl, dissolve sugar in fish sauce. Add curry powder and paste. Add pork and toss in marinade. Let stand at room temperature for at least 20 minutes, or cover and refrigerate for at least 1 hour or overnight. If refrigerated, let meat stand at room temperature for 30 minutes before cooking.

Heat oil in a wok or large, heavy frying pan over medium-high heat and add meat and marinade. Stir-fry until pork is opaque on all sides, 2–3 minutes. Add water and bring to a boil. Add ginger, peanuts, and tamarind to taste. Reduce heat to a rapid simmer and cook loin for 15 minutes. Pork butt (leg) improves with longer cooking, about 45 minutes or until tender. Pork neck will need 1 hour or longer. The sauce should slightly thicken also, for a more flavorsome, richer dish. Add more water to prevent scorching, if necessary.

Serves 4–6

Note: This dish is served in northern Thailand for ceremonial occasions such as weddings, funerals, house warmings, and temple ceremonies. If possible, use tender young ginger for the julienne in this recipe; older ginger will be more fibrous. Young ginger, which is available during summer season, is identifiable by its thin parchmentlike skin.

Ingredients

- 2 tablespoons palm sugar
- 2 tablespoons fish sauce
- 1 teaspoon curry powder or gaeng hanglay powder (see page 122)
- 3 tablespoons Hanglay curry paste (see page 84) or fresh or commercial Red curry paste (see page 60)
- 1 lb (500 g) boneless pork loin, butt (leg), or neck, trimmed and cut into 3/4-inch (2-cm) dice
- 1/4 cup (2 fl oz/60 ml) vegetable oil
- 2 cups (16 fl oz/500 ml) water
- 1 1/2-inch (4-cm) piece fresh ginger, cut into fine julienne
- 1/4 cup (1 oz/30 g) coarsely chopped roasted peanuts
- 2–3 tablespoons tamarind puree, to taste

Ingredients

FOR CURRY PASTE

15 dried long red chilies, seeded (optional)

³/₄ cup (6 fl oz/180 ml) Hanglay curry paste (see page 84) or fresh or commercial Red curry paste (see page 60)

3 tablespoons grated fresh ginger

1 teaspoon curry powder or gaeng hanglay powder (see page 122)

¹/₃ cup (25 g) chopped cilantro (fresh coriander) roots or stems (optional)

1 cup (8 fl oz/ 250 ml) water

FOR SOUPS

8 cups (64 fl oz/2 L) coconut milk

vegetable oil for deep-frying, plus 2–3 tablespoons extra

6–8 chicken legs

1 cup (8 fl oz/250 ml) chicken broth

2–3 tablespoons palm sugar

2 tablespoons granulated (white) sugar

¹/₂ cup (4 fl oz/125 ml) soy sauce

¹/₂ cup (4 fl oz/125 ml) fish sauce

1 lb (500 g) fresh egg noodles (bah mee)

FOR ACCOMPANIMENTS

about ¹/₂ cup (4 fl oz/125 ml) Chili oil (see page 118)

about 1 cup (100 g) pickled cabbage or cucumber, drained

¹/₃ cup (1 oz/30 g) quartered shallots (French shallots), preferably pink

2 limes, cut into small wedges

2 tablespoons sweet (thick) soy sauce

¹/₂ cup (¹/₂ oz/15 g) coarsely chopped cilantro (fresh coriander) leaves and stems

3 scallions (green onions), coarsely chopped

Chiang Mai noodles
Khao soi gai

To make curry paste: If using hanglay curry paste, soak dried chilies in water for 10 minutes to soften, then drain. In a blender or food processor, combine hanglay curry paste, chilies, ginger, curry powder, and cilantro. Add water and blend until smooth. If using red curry paste, only add the ginger, curry powder and puree with water in a blender, as above.

Let coconut milk stand, allowing the thick milk to rise to the top. Spoon 1 cup (8 fl oz/250 ml) thick coconut milk in a wok or large, heavy frying pan, heat for 3–5 minutes, stirring constantly, until it separates. If it does not separate, add optional oil. Add curry paste and fry, stirring constantly, until fragrant, 1–2 minutes. Add chicken, broth, remaining thick coconut milk, and half the thin coconut milk. Add palm sugar—if using a wok, add it along the edge of the wok so that it melts before stirring into the curry; if using a standard frying pan, add directly to the curry. Stir in granulated sugar, soy sauce, and fish sauce. Reduce heat to a simmer and cook, uncovered, until chicken is tender and juices run clear when it is pricked with a fork, about 30 minutes. Add water during cooking if required. Add remaining thin coconut milk and heat through.

Meanwhile, in a wok or deep-fryer, heat 3 inches (7.5 cm) oil to 350°F (185°C). Add one-fifth of noodles and cook for about 30 seconds, or until crisp. Using a skimmer, transfer to paper towels to drain. In a large pot of boiling water, cook remaining noodles in boiling water for 2 minutes; drain.

To serve, divide noodles among individual bowls. Add a chicken leg to each and ladle in curry sauce. Top with some fried noodles and serve along with bowls of accompaniments such as pickles, herbs and sauces.

Serves 6–8

Ingredients

15 dried long red chilies

1 teaspoon salt

1 stalk lemongrass, white part only, peeled and chopped

8 cilantro (fresh coriander) roots, or 2 tablespoons chopped stems

1/3 cup (1½ oz/45 g) finely chopped shallots (French shallots), preferably pink

4 large cloves garlic, crushed

2 teaspoons dried shrimp paste

Care curry paste
Nam prik gaeng care

Soak dried chilies in warm water for 10 minutes. Meanwhile, combine all remaining ingredients in a large mortar, and pound to a paste with a pestle, 10–20 minutes. Halfway through, drain the chilies, coarsely chop, then add them to the mortar and pound until well blended. Or, coarsely chop all ingredients, then put them in a food processor and process until finely chopped. If necessary, add a small amount of water, 1 teaspoon at a time (see also How to make curry bases, page 56.)

Makes about ³/₄ cup (6 fl oz/180 ml)

Hint

Make more curry paste than you need, and store the remainder for future use. Tightly covered, fresh curry paste keeps for 3–4 days in the refrigerator. Fried curry paste keeps for 2 months in the refrigerator, or indefinitely in the freezer.

Note

Making your own curry paste allows you to vary the ingredients to suit your taste: you can decrease the quantity of chilies or chili seeds, for example.

Suggested Menu

Chicken in coconut milk soup; Beef salad; Mixed vegetable curry; Steamed fish in banana leaf; Northern-style chili dipping sauce; and sticky rice.

Care curry with chicken

Gaeng care gai

In a wok or small frying pan over low heat, stir rice until golden brown, 3–5 minutes. Transfer to a mortar and pulverize with a pestle; set aside.

Heat oil in a wok or large, heavy frying pan over medium-high heat and fry curry paste, stirring constantly, until fragrant, 1–2 minutes. Add chicken and stir-fry until opaque on all sides, about 2 minutes. Add eggplants and beans; stir together well.

Add 1 cup (8 fl oz/250 ml) chicken broth or water; simmer for 2 minutes. Add remaining broth or water, fish sauce, remaining ingredients and ground rice. Bring to a boil, reduce heat, and simmer 2 minutes for chicken breasts, 5–7 minutes for thighs. Transfer to a serving bowl and serve.

Serves 4–6

Note: In Thailand, the availability of local ingredients allows for variations to this dish. For example, this recipe can be made with frog instead of chicken. If available, you can also add 1 cup dried cotton buds or kapok flowers (ngiu) at the same time as the eggplant. In the north of Thailand, 1/4 teaspoon prickly ash (kamchatton) would be added with the chicken broth. Substitute with 1/4 teaspoon Szechuan peppercorns if desired.

Ingredients

- 1 tablespoon sticky (glutinous) rice

- 1/4 cup (2 fl oz/60 ml) vegetable oil

- 1/4 cup (2 fl oz/60 ml) Care curry paste (see page 88) or fresh or commercial Red curry paste (see page 60)

- 12 oz (375 g) boneless chicken thighs or breasts, thinly sliced

- 1/2 cup (2 oz/60 g) chopped eggplant (aubergine) or 1 round eggplant or 1/4 long green eggplant

- 1/4 cup (1 oz/30 g) pea eggplants (optional)

- 2 long beans or 6–8 green beans, cut into 1-inch (2.5-cm) pieces

- 2 cups (16 fl oz/500 ml) chicken broth or water

- 2 tablespoons fish sauce

- 7 fresh eryngo (sawtooth coriander) leaves or 6 sprigs fresh cilantro (fresh coriander), coarsely chopped or torn

- 4 fresh piper (beetle) leaves, or 2 cabbage leaves, coarsely chopped

- 1 cup fresh acacia leaves, coarsely chopped (optional)

- 1 fresh long red chili, seeded and cut into large pieces

- 1/4 teaspoon salt

Ingredients

1 tablespoon sticky (glutinous) rice

¼ cup (2 fl oz/60 ml) vegetable oil

¼ cup (2 fl oz/60 ml) Care curry paste (see page 86) or fresh or commercial Red curry paste (see page 60)

1¼ cups (5 oz/150 g) chopped eggplant (aubergine) or 3 round Thai eggplants plus ½ cup (2 oz/60 g) coarsely chopped long green eggplant

¼ cup (1 oz/30 g) pea eggplants (optional)

4 long beans or 12 green beans, cut into 1-inch (2.5-cm) pieces

½ cup (2 oz/60 g) canned or 1 cup (4 oz/125 g) fresh straw mushrooms, rinsed, drained and halved

½ cup (2 oz/60 g) coarsely chopped cauliflower florets

2 cups (16 fl oz/500 ml) vegetable broth or water

2 tablespoons soy sauce or fish sauce

4 fresh piper (beetle) leaves, or 2 cabbage leaves, coarsely chopped

7 fresh eryngo (sawtooth coriander) leaves or 6 sprigs cilantro (fresh coriander), coarsely chopped or torn

1 fresh long red chili, coarsely chopped

¼ teaspoon salt

Mixed vegetable curry
Gaeng care phak ruam

In a wok or small frying pan over low heat, stir rice until golden brown, 3–5 minutes. Transfer to a mortar and pulverize with a pestle; set aside.

Heat oil in a wok or large, heavy frying pan over medium-high heat and fry curry paste, stirring constantly, until fragrant, 1–2 minutes. Add eggplants, beans, mushrooms, and cauliflower; stir together well. Add 1 cup (8 fl oz/250 ml) broth or water, and simmer for 2 minutes. Add remaining broth or water and soy or fish sauce. Bring to a boil.

Add remaining ingredients and ground rice. Bring to a boil, then reduce heat and simmer for 2 minutes. Transfer to a serving bowl and serve.

Serves 4–6

Note: In Thailand, the availability of local ingredients allows for variations to this dish. If available, you can also add 1 cup dried cotton buds or kapok flowers (ngiu) at the same time as the eggplant, and/or 1 cup chopped acacia leaves at the end. In the north of Thailand, ¼ teaspoon prickly ash (kamchatton) would be added with the chicken broth. Substitute with ¼ teaspoon Szechuan peppercorns if desired.

Steamed fish in banana leaves

Hor neung plaa

In a wok or small frying pan over low heat, stir rice until golden brown, 3–5 minutes. Transfer to a mortar and pulverize with a pestle; set aside.

Heat oil in a wok or large, heavy frying pan over medium-high heat and fry curry paste, stirring constantly, until fragrant, 1–2 minutes. Add eggplants and beans and stir well to coat. Add chicken broth or water, fish sauce, and eryngo leaves or cilantro, and bring to a boil. Add fish, stirring to coat well, then add ground rice and cook until the mixture is very thick and the fish is just opaque throughout, about 1 minute. Remove from heat.

Roll kaffir lime leaves together into a tight cylinder and cut into fine shreds. If using, wipe banana leaf with a clean cloth. Spread out each banana leaf and cut each into 8–10 pieces, 8 x 6 inches (20 x 15 cm) in size, removing the hard center stem. Center a piper leaf on each piece of banana leaf (or alternatively, cut each cabbage leaf into 8–10 small squares and place a piece on each banana leaf) and spoon about ¼ cup fish mixture on top. Sprinkle strands of shredded lime leaf over. Gently roll over sides of banana leaf, overlapping them to make a shape resembling a flat sausage. Fold or pull over 2 opposite ends to the center, and secure with a toothpick. Cook parcels in covered steamer over rapidly simmering water for about 15 minutes. Let cool slightly, then open parcels and serve on the banana leaves.

Makes 8–10

Hint: Laying a banana leaf in the sun for a couple of hours softens it slightly and makes it easier to fold. Or, run it briefly over a gas flame until it becomes waxy and very pliable. Very fresh leaves, especially young tender ones, are best. Or, use aluminum foil.

Note: This dish is ideal for picnics or at a buffet, as it is delicious eaten at room temperature. In Thailand, if available, you can also add 1 teaspoon prickly ash (kamchatton), coarsely ground, to the ground rice.

Ingredients

- 1 tablespoon sticky (glutinous) rice
- ¼ cup (2 fl oz/60 ml) vegetable oil
- ¼ cup (2 fl oz/60 ml) Care curry paste (see page 88) or fresh or commercial Red curry paste (see page 60)
- ½ cup (2 oz/60 g) chopped eggplant (aubergine) or 2 round Thai eggplants
- ¼ cup (1 oz/30 g) pea eggplants (optional)
- 4 long beans or 12 green beans, cut into ½-inch (12-mm) pieces
- ¼ cup (2 fl oz/60 ml) chicken broth or water
- 2 tablespoons fish sauce
- 8 fresh eryngo (sawtooth coriander) leaves, finely shredded, or 7 sprigs cilantro (fresh coriander), coarsely chopped
- 12 oz (375 g) firm white fish fillets such as cod, skinned and very thinly sliced
- 4 kaffir lime leaves, stemmed
- 1–2 large banana leaves (optional)
- about 10 fresh piper (beetle) leaves, or 2–3 cabbage leaves, each cut into 4 squares

Ingredients

12 oz (375 g) jumbo shrimp
(king prawns)

3 cups (24 fl oz/750 ml) chicken
broth or water

2 stalks lemongrass, white part only,
cut into 1-inch (2.5-cm) pieces

6 cloves garlic, crushed

3 tablespoons coarsely chopped
shallots (French shallots),
preferably pink

1-inch (2.5-cm) piece fresh galangal,
thinly sliced

2 firm tomatoes, cut into 8 wedges

1 cup (4 oz/125 g) canned or 2 cups
(8 oz/250 g) fresh straw
mushrooms, rinsed, drained and
halved

10 small fresh green chilies, stems
removed and halved lengthwise

2–3 tablespoons fish sauce, to taste

5 kaffir lime leaves, coarsely torn

2 tablespoons fresh lime juice

½ cup (½ oz/15 g) coarsely chopped
cilantro (fresh coriander) leaves
and stems

Tom yam soup with shrimp
Tom yam goong

Shell and devein shrimp, leaving tails intact and reserving shells and heads for the broth (see page 34). Cover and refrigerate until ready to use.

In a medium saucepan, combine shrimp heads, shells, and broth or water, and bring to a boil. Using a skimmer, remove and discard the heads and shells. Bring back to a boil. Add lemongrass, garlic, shallots, and galangal to the broth, then tomatoes, mushrooms, chilies, fish sauce to taste, and kaffir lime leaves. Simmer gently for 2 minutes then increase heat and return to a boil.

Add shrimp, and briskly boil for no more than 1 minute. Remove from heat and stir in lime juice. Transfer to bowls for serving, garnish with fresh cilantro, and serve.

Serves 4–6

Note: The fibrous ingredients in this dish—kaffir lime leaf, galangal, and lemongrass—are not eaten. Just push them aside when eating the soup. For a less spicy soup, leave the chilies whole.

Variation

Tom yam soup with chicken (Tom yam gai)
Substitute boneless, skinless chicken breast for shrimp. Cut chicken into thin strips and cook until just opaque throughout, 1–2 minutes. Continue as above.

Chicken in coconut milk soup

Tom kha gai

In a wok or large saucepan over high heat, combine coconut cream, coconut milk, lemongrass, galangal, shallots, chilies, and mushrooms. Bring to a boil, reduce heat, and simmer for 3–5 minutes. Add chicken, stirring well. Add fish sauce and lime leaves. Return to a boil. Add half the cilantro and turn off heat.

Stir in lime juice. Transfer to bowls for serving, garnish with scallions and remaining cilantro, and serve.

Serves 4–6

Hint

For a less rich soup, replace the coconut cream with an equal quantity of coconut milk. For a less spicy broth, keep the chilies whole.

Note: This is one of Thailand's best-known soups, with a creamy consistency and a lovely lemony flavor. The fibrous ingredients in this dish—kaffir lime leaf, galangal, and lemongrass—are not eaten. Just push them aside.

Ingredients

- 2 cups (16 fl oz/500 ml) coconut cream
- 1 cup (8 fl oz/125 ml) coconut milk
- 2 stalks lemongrass, white part only, peeled and cut into 1-inch (2.5-cm) pieces
- 1/2-inch (12-mm) piece galangal, thinly sliced
- 2 tablespoons coarsely chopped shallots (French shallots), preferably pink
- 10–15 small fresh chilies, halved lengthwise
- 1 cup (4 oz/125 g) canned or 2 cups (8 oz/250 g) fresh straw mushrooms, rinsed, drained and halved
- 12 oz (375 g) boneless, skinless chicken breasts, thinly sliced
- 2–3 tablespoons fish sauce, to taste
- 3 kaffir lime leaves, stemmed
- 1/2 cup (1/2 oz/15 g) coarsely chopped cilantro (fresh coriander)
- 2 tablespoons fresh lime juice
- 2 scallions (green onions), chopped

Ingredients

½ lb (250 g) beef tenderloin or sirloin, trimmed, or roast beef

salt and freshly ground pepper

1 tablespoon vegetable oil

⅓ cup (3 fl oz/90 ml) fish sauce

½ cup (4 fl oz/125 ml) fresh lime juice

about 25 fresh small green and red chilies, coarsely chopped

1 teaspoon palm sugar

1 cucumber

1 firm tomato

3 tablespoons thinly sliced shallots (French shallots), preferably pink

½ cup (2 oz/60 g) coarsely chopped Chinese or standard celery

5 scallions (green onions), cut into 1-inch (2.5-cm) pieces, including green parts

Beef **salad**
Yam neua

If using raw beef, cut into 1 or 2 thick steaks. Season lightly with salt and pepper. In a large frying pan over medium-high heat, heat oil and cook steaks for a total of 7 minutes per inch (2.5 cm) thickness, turning once, for medium rare. Remove from heat and let cool thoroughly.

In a small bowl, combine fish sauce, lime juice, chilies, and sugar. Stir until sugar is dissolved. Cut cucumber in half lengthwise, remove seeds with a spoon if desired, then cut into thin crescents. Core tomato, cut in half vertically, and slice into thin half-moons. Cut meat into thin strips, then toss with fish sauce mixture. Add cucumber, tomato, shallots, celery, and scallions, and toss to coat.

Transfer to serving dish and serve immediately.

Serves 4–6

Hint

Tender beef, such as fillet or sirloin, is best for this recipe. This is also a good way to use leftover roast beef. For a less spicy salad, leave the chilies whole and lightly bruise them before adding. Although not traditional, this salad is delicious served on a bed of greens, such as green oak leaf lettuce.

Larb salad with chicken

Larb gai

In a wok or small frying pan over low-medium heat, stir rice until golden brown, 3–5 minutes. Transfer to a mortar and pound to a coarse powder with a pestle. Transfer to a bowl and set aside. Pound galangal in the mortar until pulverized.

In a medium bowl, combine ground chicken, galangal, shallots, fish sauce, lime juice, and chili powder to taste; mix thoroughly. Heat a wok or large, heavy frying pan over medium heat and add chicken mixture all at once, stirring vigorously to keep it from sticking into lumps. Cook until opaque throughout, about 5 minutes.

Transfer to a bowl, and let cool slightly, then toss with ground rice and all remaining ingredients. If desired, garnish with additional mint leaves, and accompany with vegetable crudités, such as cabbage, carrot, cucumber, and long beans.

Serves 4–6

Hint
Ask your butcher to grind the chicken, or do it yourself in a food processor.

Variation
Larb with pork (Larb moo)
Substitute an equal quantity ground pork for chicken, and cook as above.

Ingredients

2 tablespoons sticky (glutinous) rice

2 thin slices fresh galangal

12 oz (375 g) boneless, skinless chicken breasts, ground (minced)

2 tablespoons thinly sliced shallots (French shallots), preferably pink

3 tablespoons fish sauce

2 tablespoons fresh lime juice

2–3 teaspoons chili powder, to taste

1 tablespoon coarsely chopped cilantro (fresh coriander) leaves and stems

1 scallion (green onion), including green part, coarsely chopped

1 tablespoon coarsely chopped fresh mint

Ingredients

1 lb (500 g) green papaya, peeled and seeded

3 cloves garlic, peeled

10 fresh small green chilies

2 long beans, or about 8 green beans, cut into 1-inch (2.5-cm) pieces

2 tablespoons dried shrimp

2 tablespoons fish sauce

2 tablespoons fresh lime juice

1 teaspoon palm sugar

1 tablespoon anchovy paste (optional)

1 firm tomato, coarsely chopped, or 5 cherry tomatoes, halved

2 tablespoons coarsely ground roasted peanuts

Green papaya salad
Som tom

Using a knife or shredder, shred papaya into long, thin strips. You should have about 3 cups (300–350 g); set aside. In a large mortar or bowl, combine garlic, chilies, and beans, and pound to coarsely bruise with a pestle. Add papaya and pound again to just bruise ingredients. Add dried shrimp, fish sauce, lime juice, and palm sugar. Stir together until sugar has dissolved. Add anchovy paste if using, and tomato. Gently pound to combine flavors. Transfer to a serving platter, sprinkle with peanuts, and serve.

Serves 4–6

Note: This dish is often served with steamed sticky rice and Gai yang chicken (see page 43). A complementary fresh herb, kra thin, from the lead tree, is found in many Thai markets, both in Asia and overseas. Faintly resembling acacia in appearance, it tastes similar to arugula (rocket).

Variations

If unripe or green papaya is unavailable, substitute with shredded, peeled carrot, cucumber, or melon.

Spicy cellophane noodle salad
Yam wun sen

Soak noodles in cold water for 10 minutes to soften. (If required, noodles can be prepared several hours in advance, left in the water until ready to use.) Drain and coarsely cut with scissors into 6-inch (15-cm) lengths.

In a wok or large saucepan over high heat, bring 1 cup (8 fl oz/250 ml) coconut milk or water to a boil. Add pork, stirring vigorously to break meat apart, and cook for 2 minutes. Drain, reserving ¼ cup (2 fl oz/60 ml) of the liquid. Set meat aside. In the same wok or saucepan, bring remaining coconut milk or water to a boil over high heat. Add shrimp and cook, stirring constantly, until evenly pink, about 1 minute. Drain and set shrimp aside. (If desired, reserve this cooking liquid for another dish, such as Tom yam soup with shrimp, page 94. Do not use it to flavor salad.)

In a large pot bring water to a boil, then pour boiling water into a heatproof bowl. Plunge noodles in and soak for 1 minute; drain, then soak in cold water for 1 minute. (Be precise with these timings, as you do not want the noodles to become water-logged.)

In a large bowl, combine reserved cooking liquid, fish sauce, and lime juice. Add garlic, shallots, chilies to taste, celery, tomato, and mushrooms if using. Toss together, then add noodles. Transfer to a serving plate, sprinkle cooked pork and shrimp over, garnish with fresh cilantro, and serve immediately.

Serves 4–6

Hint
Purchase individual small packets of cellophane noodles, or a packet of small bunches, as they are difficult to pry apart in large bunches. For a less spicy salad, simply bruise the whole chilies; do not cut them.

Ingredients

4 oz (125 g) cellophane (bean thread) noodles

2 cups (16 fl oz/500 ml) coconut milk or water

4 oz (125 g) ground (minced) pork

12 jumbo shrimp (king prawns), shelled and deveined

2–3 tablespoons fish sauce, to taste

2 tablespoons fresh lime juice

5 cloves pickled garlic

1 tablespoon thinly sliced shallots (French shallots), preferably pink

10–20 fresh small red chilies, thinly sliced, to taste

½ cup (2 oz/60 g) coarsely chopped celery, preferably Chinese celery

1 firm tomato, halved and thinly sliced

1 oz (30 g) fresh or dried cloud or tree ear mushrooms (black or white fungus), trimmed and rinsed, soaked if dried (optional)

½ cup (¾ oz/20 g) coarsely chopped cilantro (fresh coriander)

Ingredients

4 cups (28 oz/875 g) sticky (glutinous) rice

2 cups (16 fl oz/500 ml) coconut cream

1 cup (8 oz/250 g) granulated (white) sugar plus 2 tablespoons extra

1/2 teaspoon salt plus pinch extra

1/2 cup (4 fl oz/125 ml) coconut milk

2–3 fresh mangoes, peeled, cut from pit (stone), and thinly sliced

1 tablespoon sesame seeds, lightly toasted (see page 33)

1

2

3

SWEETS

Sweet sticky rice with mango

Khao neow mamuang

1. Put sticky rice in a large, deep bowl and add water to cover by 2 inches (5 cm). Soak for at least 3 hours, preferably 8 hours.

2. Drain, then pour rice into a conical bamboo steamer or steamer basket lined with cheesecloth (muslin). If available, place a small round bamboo mat, about 6 inches (15 cm) in diameter, into the bottom of the basket (this facilitates removal and cleaning later). Set basket over a steamer pot filled with boiling water. The basket should fit snugly deep inside the pot, but not touch the water. Cover and steam until grains are tender, about 20 minutes.

3. Halfway through the cooking, toss the rice so that it is upended. It should have already formed into a cohesive ball by this point.

In a large bowl, stir together coconut cream, sugar, and 1/2 teaspoon salt. Add hot rice, stirring until grains are well coated. Let cool completely at room temperature. (Do not refrigerate or the rice will harden.) The rice will absorb all the coconut liquid; stir occasionally. Meanwhile, in a small bowl, combine coconut milk, extra sugar, and a pinch of salt.

When ready to serve, divide sticky rice among individual serving bowls. Lay mango slices on top of sticky rice. Pour coconut milk mixture over mangoes and sprinkle with sesame seeds.

Serves 4–6

Note: If fresh mango is unavailable, use canned (tinned) mango, drained.

Black sticky rice pudding

Khao neow dam piak

Ingredients

1 cup (7 oz/220 g) black sticky rice

3½ cups (28 fl oz/875 ml) water

1 cup (8 fl oz/250 ml) coconut cream plus ¼ cup (2 fl oz/60 ml) extra

¼ cup (2 oz/60 g) granulated (white) sugar

In a medium saucepan over medium-high heat, combine rice and water and bring to a boil. Reduce heat to simmer, and cook until tender, for about 30 minutes, stirring occasionally at the beginning and frequently towards the end. Add additional water if necessary. Once the rice is just tender, and the grains begin to open, add 1 cup (8 fl oz/250 ml) coconut cream and sugar. Stir well, and cook for a few minutes more. Remove from heat. To serve, spoon pudding into individual bowls, and drizzle with extra ¼ cup (2 fl oz/60 ml) coconut cream.

Serves 4–6

Note: This recipe can be served hot, at room temperature, or chilled, but it is best when eaten on the day it is made.

Ingredients

8 unpeeled, small, slightly green, sugar bananas or 4–6 standard-sized bananas

4 cups (32 fl oz/1 L) coconut milk

2 pandan (screwpine) leaves, bruised and tied into a knot, or 2 drops pandan extract

2 tablespoons palm sugar

¼ cup (2 oz/60 g) granulated (white) sugar

pinch of salt

Bananas in coconut milk
Kluay buad chee

Cook bananas in a covered steamer over rapidly simmering water until skin begins to break, about 5 minutes. Or, cook bananas in a pot of boiling water for about 2 minutes. Remove bananas from heat, let cool slightly, then carefully peel. Cut each banana into quarters; once lengthwise, then across.

Let coconut milk stand, allowing the thick coconut milk to rise to the top. Spoon about 2 cups (16 fl oz/500 ml) of the thick milk into a bowl to reserve.

In a large saucepan over medium-high heat, combine remaining thin coconut milk and pandan leaves or extract. Bring to a boil and add banana pieces, both sugars, and salt. Add thick coconut milk, bring to a boil, and reduce heat to simmer gently for about 3 minutes. Remove from heat. Serve either hot or cold in individual bowls.

Serves 4–6

Note: Slightly green bananas work best here, as they are less likely to break up during poaching. Other alternatives include peeled and cubed pumpkin, squash, sweet potato, or taro—steam or boil until just tender, and cook as above, until tender.

Hard or loaf palm sugar is preferred in this recipe as it contains tapioca starch which slightly thickens the sauce.

Steamed banana cake

Khanom kluay

If using unsweetened dried coconut, soak first in cold water for 10 minutes, then squeeze dry. Reserve one-fourth of coconut for garnish.

In a medium bowl, mash bananas then stir in all remaining ingredients except reserved coconut. Lightly oil an 8 x 10-inch (20 x 25-cm) cake pan. Pour in cake mixture and smooth top. Sprinkle with reserved coconut. Cover tightly with plastic wrap, or lay a banana leaf on top. Place the cake in a steamer, or on a wire rack in a wok, over gently boiling water. Make sure the water does not touch the cake pan. Cover steamer, and steam for 30 minutes. Cake will be slightly springy to the touch when done.

Remove pan from the heat, and drain away any accumulated water. Let cool completely, then cut into small squares and carefully remove pieces with a spatula. Serve warm or at room temperature.

Makes 1 cake

Note: Standard servings of this cake may prove too large and heavy, so the smaller the servings, the better.

Ingredients

3 cups (12 oz/375 g) grated fresh coconut or unsweetened dried (desiccated) coconut

5 ripe bananas, about 1½ lb (750 g) in total, peeled and mashed

1 cup (5 oz/150 g) rice flour or very finely ground rice

¼ cup (1 oz/30 g) tapioca starch

1½ cups (12 oz/375 g) granulated (white) sugar

½ teaspoon salt

½ cup (4 fl oz/125 ml) coconut cream

BEVERAGES

The amount of ice added to a glass and the size of the glass will vary the number of servings possible from the measurements in this section.

Salty-sweet combinations in drinks are relished in Thailand, hence the optional inclusion of salt. To Westerners, this may be an acquired taste.

Lime **soda**
Soda maneau

Ingredients

¹/₃ **cup (3 fl oz/90 ml) fresh lime juice**

¹/₄ **cup (2 fl oz/60 ml) sugar syrup (page 114), or to taste**

pinch salt (optional)

ice

about ¹/₂ cup (4 fl oz/125 ml) soda water

In a small jug, combine lime juice, sugar syrup to taste, and salt if using. Stir to blend. Pour into a glass packed with ice. Add soda water to top off, plus additional sugar syrup if you like.

Makes about 1¹/₄ cups (10 fl oz/300 ml)

Mango **shake**
Mamuang pan

Ingredients

1 small very ripe mango (about 8 oz/250 g), peeled, cut from pit (stone), and chopped

2 tablespoons sugar syrup (page 114), or to taste

pinch salt, optional

about 1¹/₂ cups (12 oz/375 g) lightly crushed ice

¹/₂ **cup (4 fl oz/125 ml) water**

In a blender or food processor, combine all ingredients (including ice) and blend until smooth. Taste and adjust sweetening, if desired. Pour into glasses and serve immediately.

Makes about 3 cups (24 fl oz/750 ml)

Watermelon and **pineapple shake**
Teng mo kap sapparot pan

In a blender or food processor, combine all ingredients and blend until smooth. Taste and adjust sweetening, if desired. Pour into glasses and serve immediately.

Makes about 3 cups (24 fl oz/750 ml)

Ingredients

½ cup (2 oz/60 g) chopped, seeded watermelon flesh

⅓ cup (2 oz/60 g) pineapple chunks

¼ cup (2 fl oz/60 ml) sugar syrup (page 114), or to taste

about 1½ cups (12 oz/375 g) lightly crushed ice

½ cup (4 fl oz/125 ml) water

Ingredients

2 whole stalks lemongrass, including green top, coarsely chopped

3 cups (24 fl oz/750 ml) water

about 1 tablespoon sugar syrup, or to taste (see below)

ice

Lemongrass **drink**
Nam takrite

In a blender, combine lemongrass and water and blend for about 2 minutes to puree. Strain liquid through a fine-mesh sieve or cheesecloth (muslin), squeezing, or pressing with a wooden pestle, to extract all liquid.

To serve, pour lemongrass drink into glasses packed with ice and add sugar syrup, individually to each glass, to taste.

Makes 3 cups (24 fl oz/750 ml)

Ingredients

1 cup (8 oz/250 g) granulated (white) sugar

1 cup (8 fl oz/250 ml) water

Sugar **syrup**
Nam cheum

In a medium saucepan over low heat, combine sugar and water, stirring just until sugar dissolves. Once the sugar dissolves, stop stirring, increase heat, and bring the water to a boil. Continue boiling for 3 minutes without stirring. Do not let the syrup crystallize. Brush the pan side with a brush dipped in cold water. Remove from heat and let cool completely.

Pour into a jar, cover, and refrigerate indefinitely.

Makes 1$^1/_4$ cups (10 fl oz/300 ml)

Pandan drink

Nam bay toey

Ingredients

5 pandan (screwpine) leaves, cut into ½-inch (12-mm) pieces

4 cups (32 fl oz/1 L) water

2–3 tablespoons sugar syrup (see page 114), or to taste

ice

In a large saucepan over high heat, combine pandan leaves and water. Bring to boil and cook, uncovered, for about 10 minutes. Strain and let cool.

To serve, pour pandan drink into glasses packed with ice and add sugar syrup, individually to each glass, to taste.

Makes about 2 cups (16 fl oz/500 ml)

DIPS AND SAUCES

No meal is complete in Thailand without the addition of condiments such as Soybean dipping sauce (see below) and Northern-style chili dipping sauce (page 117).

Soybean dipping sauce
Lon tao jeow

Ingredients

3 stalks lemongrass, white part only, coarsely chopped

2 tablespoons coarsely chopped shallots (French shallots), preferably pink

1 fresh long red chili, coarsely chopped

2 cups (16 fl oz/500 ml) coconut cream

1/3 cup (3 fl oz/90 ml) soybean paste (bean sauce)

2 oz (60 g) ground (minced) pork

2 tablespoons palm sugar

1 tablespoon granulated (white) sugar

In a mortar, pound lemongrass, shallots and chili to a paste with a pestle; set aside. Or, slice the ingredients very thin, then chop together very finely with a cleaver or chef's knife.

In a medium saucepan over medium-high heat, bring coconut cream to a boil, stirring occasionally. Add soybean paste and cook for about 1 minute, stirring constantly. Add pork, stirring vigorously to achieve a grainy texture; it should not form into lumps. Add lemongrass, shallots, and chili; cook for another 2 minutes. Add sugars and stir until dissolved. Remove from heat, and let cool.

Serve with cooked rice and a selection of vegetable crudités.

Makes about 2¹/₂ cups (20 fl oz/625 ml)

Northern-style chili dipping sauce

Nam prik num

Ingredients

15 fresh long green chilies, roasted (page 27)

1 whole bulb garlic

9 shallots (French shallots), about 3 oz (100 g), preferably pink

1/4 teaspoon dried shrimp paste

1/2 teaspoon salt

1 tablespoon fish sauce

Peel and stem the roasted chilies but retain seeds. (For a less piquant sauce, discard some or all of the seeds.) Preheat oven to 400°F (200°C). Lightly break unpeeled garlic bulb by pressing on a knife handle with the heel of your hand, so that the cloves sit loosely together; do not separate cloves from bulb completely. Separately wrap the garlic and shallots in aluminum foil. Roast on the top shelf of the oven for about 30 minutes, or until soft to touch. Remove from oven and allow to cool to touch in foil. Peel shallots and garlic (you should have about 1/3 cup (1 1/2 oz/45 g) shallots).

In a mortar, pound chilies gently with a pestle to break them up. Add garlic, and pound briefly, then add shallots. Add shrimp paste and salt and pound again to a coarse paste. Or, pulse ingredients in a food processor. Stir in fish sauce. Serve with a selection of vegetable crudités.

Makes about 1 cup (8 fl oz/250 ml)

Ingredients

1 cup (8 fl oz/250 ml) fish sauce

1 cup (5 oz/150 g) thinly sliced, fresh medium red or green chilies

cloves from 1/2 bulb garlic, finely chopped

2–3 tablespoons fresh lime juice, to taste

Fish sauce with chilies
Nam plaa prik

In a small bowl or screw-top jar, combine all ingredients, stir or shake to blend, and serve. Refrigerate, covered, for several days.

Makes about 1^1/2 cups (12 fl oz/375 ml)

Note: This is the ubiquitous table seasoning of Thailand, used as commonly as salt and pepper. For a less spicy sauce, halve the chilies lengthwise and scrape away some or all of the seeds. Then thinly slice the chilies as above and continue.

Ingredients

3/4 cup (6 fl oz/180 ml) vegetable oil

1/2 cup dried chili flakes

Chili oil
Nam prik tort nay naman

In a well-ventilated room, heat oil in a wok or small, heavy saucepan over medium to medium-high heat, just until surface shimmers. Add chili flakes. Stir briefly and immediately remove from heat. Let cool. If tightly covered, chili oil will keep indefinitely at room temperature.

Makes about 1 cup (8 fl oz/250 ml)

Note: This chili oil is traditionally specific to Chiang Mai noodles (page 86), although it can be served with other dishes. For example, use it in Crab with yellow curry (page 40), but strain first. The chili flakes used are made from long red chilies which are less piquant than pure cayenne.

Ingredients

2 whole bulbs garlic

4 oz (125 g) shallots (French shallots), preferably pink

15 dried long red chilies

1 cup (8 fl oz/250 ml) vegetable oil

2 tablespoons palm sugar

1 tablespoon granulated (white) sugar

¼ teaspoon salt

Chili jam
Nam prik pow

Preheat oven to 400°F (200°C). Lightly break the unpeeled garlic bulb by pressing down a knife handle with the heel of your hand, so that the cloves sit loosely together, but do not separate cloves from bulb completely. Separately wrap garlic and shallots in aluminum foil. Roast on the top shelf of the oven until soft to touch, about 30 minutes. Remove from oven and allow to cool in foil. Peel shallots and garlic.

Roast chilies by tossing them in a wok or large, heavy frying pan over high heat until lightly brown, 2–3 minutes. Remove stems, but retain the seeds. In a large mortar, grind chilies to a powder with a pestle. Add roasted garlic and shallots and pound until smooth. (Or, place chilies in a food processor to grind, then add garlic and shallots and process until smooth.)

Heat oil in a wok or large, heavy frying pan over medium heat, and add chili paste. Reduce heat to low and cook for about 5 minutes, stirring frequently. Add sugars and salt, and stir until dissolved. Remove from heat.

Store in a covered jar for up to 6 months in the refrigerator. Do not drain off any oil from the top, as this helps to preserve the jam.

Makes about 1³⁄4 cups (14 fl oz/440 ml)

Note: Chili jam is served in Thailand as a table condiment, much like ketchup and mustard in the West.

Adjat sauce

Adjat

Ingredients

⅓ cup (3 oz/90 g) granulated (white) sugar

⅓ cup (3 fl oz/90 ml) water

2 tablespoons rice vinegar

¼ cup (2 oz/60 g) peeled, thinly sliced cucumber

1½ tablespoons ground roasted peanuts

1 tablespoon thinly sliced shallots (French shallots), preferably pink

1 tablespoon coarsely chopped cilantro (fresh coriander) leaves and stems

¼ fresh long red chili, coarsely chopped

In a small saucepan over low heat, combine sugar and water and stir until sugar dissolves. Increase heat, bring syrup to a full boil, and cook without stirring for a few minutes. Remove from heat and let cool. Stir remaining ingredients into syrup and serve.

Makes about ¾ cup (6 fl oz/180 ml)

Note: This sauce traditionally accompanies both Massaman and yellow curries, although it is rarely served in restaurants today. It may also be served with meat satay, but if doing so, omit the peanuts.

Sweet chili relish

Nam jim

Ingredients

2 cups (8 oz/250 g) peeled and finely shredded daikon

2 jars pickled garlic, 16 oz (500 g) each, drained and chopped

1½ cups (12 fl oz/375 ml) rice vinegar

¾ cup (1 oz/30 g) chopped cilantro (fresh coriander) roots and stems

7 fresh long red chilies, finely chopped

3¼ cups (28 oz/875 g) granulated (white) sugar

¼ teaspoon salt

In a large saucepan, combine all ingredients and slowly bring to a boil. Reduce heat, then simmer for 20 minutes. Remove from heat and let cool completely. Store in a tightly covered jar in the refrigerator for up to 1 month.

Makes about 5 cups (36 fl oz/1.25 L)

Note: To save time, prepare ingredients that require chopping in a food processor.

Hint
This sauce is fast becoming a standard table condiment in the West. Traditionally, it accompanies Fish cakes (page 66), grilled or fried dishes such as Chicken with lemongrass (page 43), and squid rings and spring rolls.

Glossary

Acacia (Sha'om) Pungent-smelling feathery light-green leaves, with a spiky stalk and sometimes tiny white flowers. Available in Southeast Asian markets. Pods are also common in Thai markets.

Anchovy paste A thick, Western sauce made from pounded salted anchovies. Available in tubes in supermarkets and specialty food stores. This is the closest substitute to the popular Thai condiment "pla rah" or "rotten fish."

Banana leaf (Bai dtong kluay) Available from Asian greengrocers and markets. Choose young, flexible leaves if possible. Wipe the leaves before using, and tear or cut them into the desired size. Laying banana leaves in the sun for a few hours helps soften them prior to folding, as does running them briefly over a gas flame until the milky (waxy) side becomes shiny.

Chili oil (Nam prik tort nay naman) Available at most Asian markets and many Western markets. Make sure that the base oil is not toasted sesame oil, lest its taste dominates. Chili oil is easily made at home (page 118).

Cilantro (fresh coriander/Phak chee) The strong-tasting roots are pounded into curry pastes, but stems may be substituted. The leaves are a standard garnish. Also known as Chinese parsley.

Coconut milk and cream (Gati) Make sure not to buy sweetened coconut milk or "cream of coconut" which is also sweetened. Generally speaking, the less liquid in the can, the richer the coconut cream or milk. Do not shake cans before using. Rather, open carefully, stand and let the thick milk rise to the top before spooning it off to measure. Coconut milk can also be made from dried coconut, but is less satisfactory.

Cotton buds (Dork ngiu heng) The dried flowers from the kapok tree. While there is no distinct smell, its taste is reminiscent of okra. If unavailable, omit.

Cucumber (Teng) There are two kinds of Thai cucumbers, the shorter teng kwha variety, and the longer teng laan. Try to buy small Lebanese-style cucumbers, or use English (hothouse) cucumbers. Peeling is optional, but the seeds are generally eaten.

Curry paste (Nam prik) A combination of pounded chilies, either dried or fresh, herbs, and spices. Red, green and yellow curry pastes are commercially prepared; the best of these are refrigerated, frozen, or sold in sealed plastic packs or tubs on counter shelves. Jars and cans are less flavorful, due to the varying degrees of heat in packaging.

Curry powder (Pong khruang gaeng) There is no standard definition for Thai curry powder, although most Indian-style curry powders will do. A fairly standard blend for gaeng hanglay curry powder (pong gaeng hanglay) can be used in most Thai dishes (see page 85). To make, combine equal amounts of cumin seeds, ground turmeric, ground coriander seeds, and mace. In a small, dry pan, lightly toast the spices, stirring constantly, until fragrant. Let cool, grind together in a mortar or spice grinder, then store in an airtight jar in a dark place for up to 6 months.

Daikon (Hua chai tao) A long, thick "giant" white radish, principally associated with Japan. Choose a firm, crisp specimen, and peel before using.

Fish sauce (Nam pla) Fish sauce is made from the fermented extract of salted small fish. It is used both as a table condiment and in the kitchen. Once opened, used within 1 month or refrigerate for up to 6 months. After that, the flavor rapidly deteriorates. (See also Ingredients, page 19).

Flour, all-purpose (plain) Wheat flour is rarely used in Thai cooking, except when coating certain foods for deep-frying, such as Fried fish with Penang sauce (page 82). The distinct crust is not achievable with tapioca starch or cornstarch (cornflour).

Garlic, pickled (Grathiam dong) Used in yam salads, or to accompany khao soi noodles (page 86). Available from Asian grocery stores.

Lead tree (Kra thin) A long spindly green, with a flavor similar to arugula (rocket). While it faintly resembles acacia in appearance, it does not have a strong odor. It is generally eaten raw, as an accompaniment to Green papaya salad (page 102), chili-based dipping sauces, and peanut-based curries or satays.

Mace (Dawk chand) A spice obtained from the outer covering of the nutmeg. It is avaiable whole (in "blades" or pieces) and ground.

Mushrooms, straw (Hed fang) Straw mushrooms are sold canned or dried, and occasionally fresh. Rinse and drain mushrooms before using. When using canned mushrooms, reduce the quantity in the recipe by half.

Mushrooms, tree ear or cloud (black or white fungus/Hed hunu) These add texture, but little taste, to food, but absorb flavors during cooking. The dried mushrooms must be soaked in water to rehydrate, then rinsed thoroughly and drained. Trim the tough stems from the fresh or dried mushrooms before using.

Noodles Dried rice noodles are brittle and should be broken into the desired size, then soaked until tender. They are added to soups and stir-fries. Unsoaked dried rice noodles can also be deep-fried as a crisp garnish. Cellophane noodles, also known as bean thread vermicelli or glass noodles, are made from mung bean starch. They also need soaking, but are otherwise not interchangeable. Because of their toughness, soak them prior to cutting. Wheat noodles should not be soaked. Boil them until tender then drain and reserve; quickly refresh in boiling water before using (see also Ingredients, pages 20–21). The following are popular noodle varieties: vermicelli-thin rice noodles (sen mee); thin vermicelli made from mung beans (woo sen); noodles about the width of a bean sprout (sen lek); wide rice noodles, often stir-fried (sen yai); generic rice noodles (guay tiaw); medium-thin egg and wheat noodle (bah mee).

Oyster sauce (Naman hoi) A thick Chinese sauce used similarly to soy sauce, but always in cooked dishes; it is not served as a table condiment. Its taste is faintly reminiscent of oysters.

Pepper, long (Phrik haang) This pepper resembles a tiny pine cone, up to 1½ inches (4 cm) long. Floral smelling, they are numbingly hot. When unavailable, omit, or slightly increase the quantity of black pepper.

Piper leaf (beetle leaf/Bai chaa phluu) Similarly shaped, but larger and less shiny than the betel nut leaf (which is hot and peppery, the Asian equivalent of chewing tobacco). The similarity of the two leaves leads to all sorts of confusion, hence piper leaves are commonly called "beetle leaf" as well as "pepper leaf." Fresh piper leaves are used to wrap individual portions of food before popping them into the mouth. They can also be used as a canapé base. Piper leaves can be purchased fresh in Southeast Asian markets but if unavailable, either omit, or substitute a small piece of cabbage leaf. (See also Ingredients, page 22.)

Prickly ash (Makhwen or kamchatton) Tiny dried fruit of a large-canopied tree, the spice smells similar to a blend of Szechuan peppercorns and white peppercorns, but tastes hotter. Prickly ash commonly flavors Thai salads, some sour dishes, and curries, particularly in the north of Thailand. If unavailable, omit or use ground white pepper or Szechuan peppercorns.

Rice (Khao) The principal rice in Thailand is long-grain jasmine. Substitute any long-grain variety. Short-grain versions of sticky (glutinous) rice, sometimes labeled "sweet rice," are popular in China and Japan but Thais prefer a long-grain sticky rice variety. (See Ingredients, pages 22–23.)

Shrimp paste, dried (Kapi) Available at Asian grocery stores, dried shrimp paste is sold unrefrigerated, often under its Malaysian name "balachan." It is usually in a paper-wrapped bar form, but it also comes in cans and jars. It keeps indefinitely, but once open, it should be sealed tightly. In Asia, shrimp paste is usually roasted prior to flavoring dishes. However, if this aroma is too strong, then this step is optional. For the intrepid, wrap the shrimp paste in foil and place under the broiler (grill) for 2 minutes on each side, or until fragrant. Or, bake the foil-wrapped packets in a preheated hot oven for 20–30 minutes.

Soy sauce (Saut tua luang) Thai soy sauces are made in a range of strengths, progressively labeled from 1–6 in degree of strength. Japanese light soy sauce is called "usukuchi," and is similar to common Thai soy sauce (sieuw khaw). As a rule, Chinese light soy sauce is equal to dark (or regular) Japanese soy sauce. Another variety is thick (sweet) soy sauce (sieuw dam), and this is equivalent to the Indonesian ketjap manis. In all types, the flavor of naturally brewed soy sauce is best. Use soy sauce within 1 month of opening, or keep refrigerated for up to 6 months.

Star anise (Poy kak or dok chan) Although similar in smell to the anise herb, this spice bears no relation. Identifiable by its eight-arched pods, forming a star, it is the dominant flavor in Chinese Five Spice powder.

Sugar, palm (Nam taan beep) Although largely interchangeable, there are two kinds of palm sugar: one from the coconut tree (nam taan maprow), and the other, more commonly from the palm (nam taan taan tanodt). It is sometimes also known as "date sugar." The sap of either tree is boiled until thick, then bottled in a slightly gooey state (soft palm sugar), or blended with tapioca flour and formed into hard mounds. Hard palm sugar must be shaved with a knife before using.

Sugar, granulated or white (Nam taan oiy) Granulated cane sugar, although sugar-beet sugar is comparable. Dark, hardened logs of the cane sugar are also used to achieve a sweeter taste than palm sugar.

Tamarind (Ma kham) Tamarind puree, sold in jars, is available on supermarket shelves. Because there can be a difference in sourness, quantities required are slightly variable.

Water spinach (morning glory/Pak bong) In Thailand, this fresh vegetable comes in two sorts: "pak bong jiin," or the Chinese style, which has long green leaves on a green stalk; and the "Thai pak bong" which has broader ivy-like leaves and thicker stems. Their flavors are similar, but the Chinese-style is more commonly available outside of Thailand. Chop and stir-fry, or serve the tender shoots raw (see Green papaya salad, page 102).

Winged bean (Thua phuu) A four-sided green bean with frilly edges along each side. Older beans require stringing, but otherwise can be eaten raw or blanched. Substitute with long or green beans.

Index

Guide to weights and measures

The conversions given in the recipes in this book are approximate. Whichever system you use, remember to follow it consistently, thereby ensuring that the proportions are consistent throughout a recipe.

WEIGHTS

Imperial	Metric
⅓ oz	10 g
½ oz	15 g
¾ oz	20 g
1 oz	30 g
2 oz	60 g
3 oz	90 g
4 oz (¼ lb)	125 g
5 oz (⅓ lb)	150 g
6 oz	180 g
7 oz	220 g
8 oz (½ lb)	250 g
9 oz	280 g
10 oz	300 g
11 oz	330 g
12 oz (¾ lb)	375 g
16 oz (1 lb)	500 g
2 lb	1 kg
3 lb	1.5 kg
4 lb	2 kg

VOLUME

Imperial	Metric	Cup
1 fl oz	30 ml	
2 fl oz	60 ml	¼
3 fl oz	90 ml	⅓
4 fl oz	125 ml	½
5 fl oz	150 ml	⅔
6 fl oz	180 ml	¾
8 fl oz	250 ml	1
10 fl oz	300 ml	1¼
12 fl oz	375 ml	1½
13 fl oz	400 ml	1⅔
14 fl oz	440 ml	1¾
16 fl oz	500 ml	2
24 fl oz	750 ml	3
32 fl oz	1 L	4

USEFUL CONVERSIONS

¼ teaspoon	1.25 ml
½ teaspoon	2.5 ml
1 teaspoon	5 ml
1 Australian tablespoon	20 ml (4 teaspoons)
1 UK/US tablespoon	15 ml (3 teaspoons)

OVEN TEMPERATURE GUIDE

The Celsius (°C) and Fahrenheit (°F) temperatures in this chart apply to most electric ovens. Decrease by 25°F (10°C) for a gas oven or refer to the manufacturer's temperature guide. For temperatures below 325°F (160°C), do not decrease the given temperature.

Oven description	°C	°F	Gas Mark
Cool	110	225	¼
	130	250	½
Very slow	140	275	1
	150	300	2
Slow	170	325	3
Moderate	180	350	4
	190	375	5
Moderately Hot	200	400	6
Fairly Hot	220	425	7
Hot	230	450	8
Very Hot	240	475	9
Extremely Hot	250	500	10